The Economics of Analytics, and Digital Transformation

The theorems, laws, and empowerments to
guide your organization's digital transformation

Bill Schmarzo

BIRMINGHAM - MUMBAI

The Economics of Data, Analytics, and Digital Transformation

Copyright © 2020 Packt Publishing

Producer: Tushar Gupta
Content Development Editors: Bhavesh Amin and Edward Doxey
Technical Editor: Karan Sonawane
Project Editor: Mrunal Dave
Proofreader: Safis Editing
Indexer: Tejal Soni
Presentation Designer: Sandip Tadge

First published: November 2020

Production reference: 1261120

Published by Packt Publishing Ltd.
Livery Place
35 Livery Street
Birmingham B3 2PB, UK.

ISBN 978-1-80056-1410

www.packt.com

Pack<t>

packt.com

Subscribe to our online digital library for full access to over 7,000 books and videos, as well as industry leading tools to help you plan your personal development and advance your career. For more information, please visit our website.

Why subscribe?

- Spend less time learning and more time coding with practical eBooks and Videos from over 4,000 industry professionals
- Learn better with Skill Plans built especially for you
- Get a free eBook or video every month
- Fully searchable for easy access to vital information
- Copy and paste, print, and bookmark content

Did you know that Packt offers eBook versions of every book published, with PDF and ePub files available? You can upgrade to the eBook version at www.Packt.com and as a print book customer, you are entitled to a discount on the eBook copy. Get in touch with us at customercare@packtpub.com for more details.

At www.Packt.com, you can also read a collection of free technical articles, sign up for a range of free newsletters, and receive exclusive discounts and offers on Packt books and eBooks.

Foreword

In today's digital era, every organization has data, and by the ton! Having a lot of data is neither a market discriminator for an organization, nor is it a bragging point anymore (if that ever made sense anyway). The real market discriminators are an organization's data-fueled analytics products that inspire innovation, deliver insights, inform actionable decisions, generate value, and produce mission success for the organization. **Data Analytics** should first and foremost be about action and value. Consequently, the great value of this book is that it seeks to be actionable. It is not offering a set of static lecture points on analytics that you can sit and reflect upon, but it offers a dynamic progression of purpose-driven ignition points that should lift you out of your seat and that you can act upon. Bill Schmarzo is the perfect author to deliver such analytics insights through this book. He is an experienced, influential, and inspiring exemplar of data analytics leadership, and those characteristics are evident throughout its pages and chapters.

By directly addressing the economics of data, analytics, and digital transformation, Bill affirms one of the greatest defining characteristics of data. Data is not a typical business asset that depletes and depreciates with use. Its economic value is far greater and more interesting than that. Data is a renewable and reusable source, essentially never depleted (at least not depleted in a business cycle lifetime). Data can be used and reused for countless different applications, without diminishing its economic value. The use cases may have varying levels of value, which need to be assessed and evaluated, and that is exactly the theme for most of this book's chapters. We also learn that data is not only a renewable source of value, with essentially zero marginal cost for new applications, but data is also a source for asset creation that appreciates in value.

Clear steps toward achieving actionable insights, discovery from data, economic value from analytics, and forward progress toward true digital transformation are the invaluable contributions of this book. But let us not forget the marvelous collection of infographics that accompany these rich concepts. Anyone who has read Bill's articles will recognize his style of infographics and will know what a great source of knowledge they are. As someone once said (it was me, actually), "a word is worth one milli-picture." Consequently, one can be justified in and forgiven for initially skipping the words and instead first looking at the pictures in this book. They give true meaning to the label "infographic," for they contain a wealth of information, knowledge, lessons learned, and actionable insights too. They also serve as invaluable anchors to the key concepts, theorems, and performance indicators described in the various chapters, thus firmly planting each important lesson in a memorable visual context.

While there are many data analytics books available on the market, many of which help you learn concepts, applications, and use cases, this book goes beyond one-shot learning. The focus here is correctly on continuous learning, not just concepts about data, but learning continuously from data—rapidly and effectively in an agile culture of innovation and experimentation! That is what machine learning is all about and what data science is—inferring, learning, refining, and relearning! As Bill says, "*Data science is about identifying variables and metrics that might be better predictors of performance.*" That is an experimental (scientific) process that involves data! Data science is only of value to a business when it creates business value. Some analytics and data science projects fail because they are isolated projects (perhaps science experiments) for the R&D department, and thus are not an integral component of business decisions, enterprise planning, and corporate mission. Continuous learning requires humility, empowered teams, and explicit corporate recognition of this truth: "If you aren't failing enough, then you're not learning enough."

One thing that a scientific process does is to separate failed hypotheses and predictions from successful ones. Bill addresses this also, within its business context, when he describes how some organizations fail in their analytics programs due to having too many use cases, not from the lack of use cases. These organizations have not used analytics on their analytics program itself. This meta-approach expertly guides you through the theorems, data asset valuations, and economic principles presented in a unique style throughout this book. The Data Science Value Engineering Framework will steer organizations toward lean, efficient, and effective analytics innovations, outcomes, and mission successes. That might require some unlearning to get started with and to get right, but most learning starts with unlearning. As Bill says, "*Be prepared to let go of outdated approaches to learn new ones.*" This book will guide you and inspire you in that data analytics learning journey!

Dr. Kirk Borne

Data Scientist and Executive Advisor, Booz Allen Hamilton

Contributor

About the author

Bill Schmarzo, The Dean of Big Data, is a University of San Francisco School of Management Executive Fellow and an Honorary Professor at the School of Business and Economics at the National University of Ireland-Galway, where he teaches and mentors students in his courses "Big Data MBA" and "Thinking Like a Data Scientist." He is the author of *Big Data: Understanding How Data Powers Big Business*, *Big Data MBA: Driving Business Strategies with Data Science*, and *The Art of Thinking Like a Data Scientist*. He has written countless whitepapers, articles, and blogs, and has given keynote presentations and university lectures on the topics of data science, artificial intelligence/machine learning, data economics, design thinking, and team empowerment.

Thanks to Lisa Mae DeMasi and Arielle Winchester for their continued support and for energizing me with their creative ideas. Arielle is one of the most talented graphical designers I've ever seen because of her ability to turn my blogs into visual stories. And Lisa Mae understands my writing style better than me, as she critiques and enhances all of my blogs, like what she's done with this book. I can see a ghostwrite in the future!

Thanks to my family—Carolyn, Alec, Max, and Amelia—who not only provide support for my endeavors but are constantly opening my eyes to new ways of thinking about some of today's most challenging cultural and social challenges. They are an inspiration to me every day in their fearlessness.

Thanks to Professor Mouwafac Sidaoui (formerly of the University of San Francisco, but now the Dean of the School of Business at Menlo College) and Professor Denis Dennehy (Lecturer in Business Information Systems at the School of Business & Economics at the National University of Ireland-Galway). Both of them have pushed me out of my comfort zone into the world of academics, and for that, I will always be grateful. I simply cannot imagine my life without teaching, as there is nothing that I do that is as enjoyable and energizing as teaching.

I want to say thanks to my Hitachi Vantara teammates: Mauro, Yong, Ain, Jiayi, Mohan, Hareesh, Matt, Nelson, Lainey, Kelly, Zach, Jens, Ken, Mark, Kim, Sharon, and Rebecca. Every day they teach me something new or are challenging me to let go of old, outdated concepts so that I can learn again.

And finally, special thanks to dearest friends—Josh Siegel, Wei Lin, and John Morley. They were my first-round draft choices when I came over to Hitachi Vantara, and I am honored that they decided to join me on this adventure (think Jason and the Argonauts...the old version, not the sucky new version). I have worked with these guys for nearly ten years now, and I truly believe that as long as I can continue to work with them, I will never retire.

TABLE OF CONTENTS

BILL SCHMARZO
Dean of Big Data

Preface

The COVID-19 pandemic has been exacerbated by incomplete and opaque data supporting suspect analytics, economic turbulence despite trillions of dollars spent in overly generalized financial interventions, and civil unrest from years of ineffective blanket policy decisions. The ability to uncover and leverage the nuances in data to make more effective and informed policy, operational, and economic decisions is more important than ever. However, improving decisions in a world of constant change will only happen if we create a culture of continuous exploring, learning, and adapting. Only when the learnings gleaned from detailed data can be quickly codified, disseminated, and assimilated will we drive more accurate and more relevant policy and operational decisions.

To evolve our society—that is, to improve welfare, healthcare, housing, education, employment, and the environment—requires a culture of continuous learning. Our ability to evolve our society rests on this simple but overwhelmingly powerful observation:

The economies of learning are more powerful than the economies of scale.

Data is a four-letter word that has enormous transformative potential. It's the superhero of the future. But data without analytics is an empty promise. There is no value in just having data. The value of data is only realized when you apply analytics to uncover the insights that can improve healthcare effectiveness, reduce unplanned operational downtime, decrease customer attrition, increase educational opportunities, reduce operational costs, reduce traffic accidents, improve college retention, reduce deaths associated with cancer, and build winning sports teams. Yes, data and analytics can do all that...and much much more!

The material in this timely book seeks to stitch together my blog and lecture points in a coherent, cohesive and actionable manner that conveys the pragmatic and actionable concepts refined from customer engagements. As the reader, I invite you—nay, urge you—to take what I've learned and build upon it.

Throughout the book, I will challenge the reader to bear in mind: *If you want to change the game, change the frame.* I encourage you to let go of outdated concepts, and adopt a new mindset about how organizations can leverage data and analytics to derive and drive new sources of value; a mindset that seeks to exploit "The Economics of Data, Analytics, and Digital Transformation."

The book begins with two foundational chapters that I have covered extensively in other books, but the concepts are so fundamental in helping organizations leverage data and analytics to drive their digital transformation that to omit them would leave the book incomplete and of less actionable value. If nothing else, this book seeks to be actionable!

I invite you to grasp hold of the concepts in this book to thrive in the digital future. Applying the knowledge to leverage the economics of data, analytics, and digital transformation to create a culture—a society—that can continuously learn and adapt is how we'll transform our society.

Finally, let's keep learning together because, at the end of the day, we stand on one another's shoulders. If we don't work together to lead social evolution leveraging the economics of data, analytics, and digital transformation, then who will?

What this book covers

Chapter 1, The CEO Mandate: Become Value-driven, Not Data-driven, covers the Big Data Business Model Maturity Index and how organizations can become more effective at leveraging data and analytics to power their business models. It discusses the five stages of the Big Data Business Model Maturity Index—Business Monitoring, Business Insights, Business Optimization, Insights Monetization, and Digital Transformation—and provides a best-in-industry benchmark against which organizations can compare themselves (so that they know what "*good*" looks like), as well as a roadmap for how organizations can become more effective at leveraging data and analytics.

Chapter 2, Value Engineering: The Secret Sauce for Data Science Success, entails my Data Science Value Engineering Framework, a process that starts with a thorough understanding of the organization's key business initiatives, or what the organization is trying to achieve from a business or operational perspective. The Data Science Value Engineering process identifies and interrogates the key stakeholders to identify their top priority use cases (clusters of decisions around a common subject area) that support the business initiative. Once you have identified, validated, valued, and prioritized the use cases, then the supporting data, analytics, architecture, and technology requirements fall out as a consequence of the process.

Chapter 3, A Review of Basic Economic Concepts, is about Economics— the branch of knowledge concerned with the production, consumption, and transfer of wealth or value. Economics provides the framework that we will use to ascertain the value of the organization's data. Also, economics plays a huge role in justifying the game-changing potential of composable, reusable, continuously learning analytic modules. We will review some fundamental economic concepts, such as the Economic Value Curve, the Economic Multiplier Effect, Price Elasticity, the Economic Utility Function, and the Law of Supply and Demand, and discuss the applicability of those economic concepts to the world of data and analytics.

Chapter 4, University of San Francisco Economic Value of Data Research Paper, is the heart of the book and covers the research paper that Professor Mouwafac Sidaoui and I wrote while at the University of San Francisco on determining the value of data. During this research project, my initial frame of thinking was transformed by a simple statement by a research assistant—that data was an unusual asset that never wore out, never depleted, and could be applied against an unlimited number of use cases at a near-zero marginal cost. That's when I realized that determining the value of data wasn't an accounting exercise; it was an economics exercise. Yep, lots of "unlearning" for me!

Chapter 5, The Economic Value of Data Theorems, discusses the Economic Value of Data learning that I have observed since the release of that research paper. I introduce several Economic Value of Data "Theorems" that organizations can use to guide their data, analytic, and human investments to derive and drive new sources of customer, product, and operational value.

Chapter 6, The Economics of Artificial Intelligence, builds on one of the key inhibitors to the Economic Value of Data that we uncovered in the research paper—orphaned analytics. Since the completion of the USF research project, two companies have totally transformed my thinking about the game-changing potential of leveraging **Artificial Intelligence (AI)** to create analytic assets that appreciate, not depreciate, in value the more that they are used. This is truly an eye-opening chapter!

Chapter 7, The Schmarzo Economic Digital Asset Valuation Theorem, builds upon the economic aspects of data and analytics covered in the previous chapters to create the "Schmarzo Economic Digital Assets Valuation Theorem." I drill into the concepts that support the theorem and provide detailed examples as to how it works. Hopefully, this work will be sufficient to convince the Royal Swedish Academy of Sciences that I am worthy of a Nobel Prize in Economics (otherwise, I'll just have to settle with having written this book instead).

Chapter 8, The 8 Laws of Digital Transformation, brings together the data and analytic concepts from the other chapters to create the Digital Transformation roadmap, including the "laws" that guide an organization's digital transformation. And while this chapter may be a wee bit presumptive (since organizations actually will never complete their digital transformations), it will provide guidance as to what some organizations can do today to further their digital transformation.

Chapter 9, Creating a Culture of Innovation Through Empowerment, concludes the book with a focus on the role of empowering teams to drive sustainable and continuous digital transformation. This may be the most important chapter in the book because if you haven't empowered your teams, then no amount of data and analytics will make a difference in your digital transformation. I'll give examples about how organizations can empower teams that strive toward the Best "Best Options" (instead of settling for the Least "Worst Options") on the path to scaling innovation.

Appendix A, My Most Popular Economics of Data, Analytics, and Digital Transformation Infographics, includes my most popular infographics. Infographics are a great communication tool; the modern storyteller's weapon to give difficult and provocative ideas voice and make them come to life. I hope that you enjoy these infographics as much as I do.

Appendix B, The Economics of Data, Analytics, and Digital Transformation Cheat Sheet, provides a cheat sheet summary of all the chapters.

Throughout the book, several fundamental enablers repeat—Analytic Profiles and Digital Twins as critical analytic assets; composable, reusable, continuously learning analytic modules; a use case-by-use case approach for valuing and building one's data and analytic assets; and the data lake as a collaborative value creation platform. These are the connective tissue that ties everything together and forms the basis for understanding and mastering the economics of data, analytics, and digital transformation.

I hope you enjoy the book and remember *if you want to change the game, change the frame.*

Download the color images

We also provide a PDF file that has color images of the screenshots/diagrams used in this book. You can download it here: `https://static.packt-cdn.com/downloads/9781800561410_ColorImages.pdf`

Conventions used

There are a number of text conventions used throughout this book.

Bold: Indicates a new term, an important word, or words that you see on the screen, for example, in menus or dialog boxes, also appear in the text like this. For example: "Develop a **Business Case** with financial and business justification and supporting **Return on Investment** (**ROI**) analysis."

 Tips and tricks appear like this.

Get in touch

Feedback from our readers is always welcome.

General feedback: Email `feedback@packtpub.com`, and mention the book's title in the subject of your message. If you have questions about any aspect of this book, please email us at `questions@packtpub.com`.

Errata: Although we have taken every care to ensure the accuracy of our content, mistakes do happen. If you have found a mistake in this book we would be grateful if you would report this to us. Please visit, `http://www.packtpub.com/submit-errata`, selecting your book, clicking on the Errata Submission Form link, and entering the details.

Piracy: If you come across any illegal copies of our works in any form on the Internet, we would be grateful if you would provide us with the location address or website name. Please contact us at copyright@ packtpub.com with a link to the material.

If you are interested in becoming an author: If there is a topic that you have expertise in and you are interested in either writing or contributing to a book, please visit http://authors.packtpub.com.

Reviews

Please leave a review. Once you have read and used this book, why not leave a review on the site that you purchased it from? Potential readers can then see and use your unbiased opinion to make purchase decisions, we at Packt can understand what you think about our products, and our authors can see your feedback on their book. Thank you!

For more information about Packt, please visit packtpub.com.

BILL SCHMARZO
Dean of Big Data

1

THE CEO MANDATE: BECOME VALUE-DRIVEN, NOT DATA-DRIVEN

"Data is the new oil."

For the first time in my long tenure in the data and analytics business, the world has started to associate "value" to data. In fact, *The Economist* on their May 6, 2017 magazine cover declared, "The world's most valuable resource is no longer oil, but data," validating the digital future and putting an end to the way most organizations have previously regarded data in its collection, storage and associated reporting—as a necessary cost of doing business and one to be minimized, at that.

But what does "data is the new oil" really mean and how will it impact organizations?

In the same way that oil fueled the economic growth of the 20th century, data will be the catalyst for the economic growth of the 21st century. That data, including **Big Data** and **Internet of Things (IoT)** data, coupled with advanced analytics, such as **Artificial Intelligence (AI)**, **Machine Learning (ML)**, and **Deep Learning (DL)**, will be the guiding and differentiating force that drives an organization's business and operational success, and ultimately, their digital transformation.

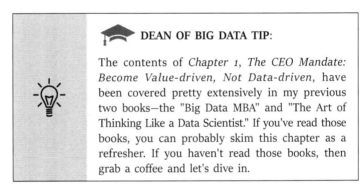

DEAN OF BIG DATA TIP:

The contents of *Chapter 1, The CEO Mandate: Become Value-driven, Not Data-driven*, have been covered pretty extensively in my previous two books—the "Big Data MBA" and "The Art of Thinking Like a Data Scientist." If you've read those books, you can probably skim this chapter as a refresher. If you haven't read those books, then grab a coffee and let's dive in.

The Data- and Value-Driven Mindsets, Defined

I often hear Senior Executives state that they want to become data-driven as if somehow having data is valuable in itself. The value of data isn't in just having it (data-driven). The value of data is determined by how you use it to create new sources of value (**value-driven**). To exploit the economic potential of data, Senior Executives must transition from a data-driven mindset (focused on amassing data) to a value-driven mindset (focused on exploiting the data to derive and drive new sources of customer, product and operational value).

Data may be the new oil or the most valuable resource in the world, but it is the *customer, product and operational analytic* insights *(propensities) buried in the data that will determine the winners and losers in the 21ˢᵗ century.*

 DEAN OF BIG DATA TIP:

Whenever I use the term **"insights"** in the book, I will also add the term **"propensities"** to reflect the predictive nature of insights. "Propensities" are an inclination or natural tendency for customers, products and operations to behave or act in a predictable way.

Consequently, if organizations are ready to embrace that "data is the new oil" and "data is the most valuable resource in the world," then the single most important question the organization must answer is:

"How effective is our organization at leveraging data and analytics to power our business and operational models?"

In this digitally-transforming world, the only sustainable and defensible differentiation is an organization's ability to exploit the economic value of its data and analytic assets to deliver analytics-infused customer, product, service and operational outcomes. It won't be the technology platform (whose differentiation is quickly eroded) and it won't be the user interface (which is easy to replicate in this digital-centric world). No, *the source of sustainable, competitive differentiation will be the organization's ability to uncover superior customer, product, service, and operational insights, and interweave those insights into the organization's operational systems and value creation processes.*

DEAN OF BIG DATA TIP:

I am going to introduce several concepts and ideas in this chapter that will be covered in more detail later on in the book.

Let's put the matter into context for your organization. How is your organization leveraging data and analytics to:

- Optimize key operational and business processes?

- Mitigate security, compliance and management risks?

- Uncover new sources of customer, product, operational and market revenue?

- Create a more differentiated, compelling customer experience?

Most organizations have no idea how to answer these questions because they lack a "best-in-industry" benchmark against which to compare themselves. Organizations need this benchmark to:

- Compare and assess their performance against the best-in-industry from a data and analytics usage perspective.

- Provide a simple and actionable roadmap to become more effective at leveraging data and analytics.

- Envision what "good" might look like for their organization.

The "Big Data Business Model Maturity Index" is a framework that I created to help organizations:

1. Map or benchmark where they sit today in comparison to data and analytics "best-in-industry" practices, and

2. Provide a roadmap for becoming more effective at leveraging data and analytics to power the organization's business models (see *Figure 1.1*).

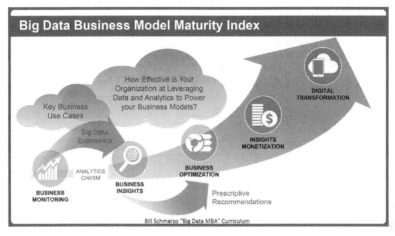

Figure 1.1: The Big Data Business Model Maturity Index

Figure 1.1 is the core of this book. If you don't understand what "good" looks like from a data and analytics perspective—if you don't know how far you can push your organization to exploit the business potential of data and analytics—then how is your organization ever going to master the economics of data, analytics and digital transformation? The mastery of the economics of data, analytics and digital transformation is what will distinguish the winners from the losers in the 21st century! Yes, mastering *Figure 1.1* is a matter of survival.

Understanding the Big Data Business Model Maturity Index Phases

Let's deep dive into each phase of the **Big Data Business Model Maturity Index (BDBMMI)**.

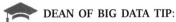

DEAN OF BIG DATA TIP:

From an advanced analytics perspective, Phase 1 of the BDBMMI leverages Descriptive and Exploration analytics to tell you what happened and why. Phases 2 and 3 of the BDBMMI leverage **Predictive Analytics** (to predict what is likely to happen) and **Prescriptive Analytics** (to prescribe preventative or recommended actions based upon the predictive analytics). Phase 5 leverages Automation and Autonomous analytics to create a business and operating model that is continuously learning and adapting to environmental and industry changes.

Phase 1: Business Monitoring: The Business Monitoring phase seeks to **monitor** and report on "What's Happened?" with respect to the operations of the business. The Business Monitoring phase is where companies leverage **Business Intelligence (BI)** and data warehouses to generate management and operational reports and dashboards that communicate current operational status. The Business Monitoring phase leverages rudimentary analytics such as benchmarking (against previous periods, industry benchmarks, and plan) and indices (brand development, customer satisfaction, product performance, financials) to identify or flag under- and over-performing business areas that require more management or operational attention.

Unfortunately, running your business on retrospective reports and dashboards that tell the organization "What's Happened?" is like trying to drive your car using the rear-view mirror. It is easy for organizations to get lackadaisical and declare "mission accomplished" at the completion of this phase. And while the Business Monitoring phase is a great starting point, on its own the Business Monitoring phase is insufficient in helping organizations to become more effective at leveraging data and analytics to power their business models.

Organizations must push beyond this phase if they seek to become more predictive and prescriptive in optimizing the operations of the business. And that means running smack into the dreaded **Analytics Chasm**.

First off, the Analytics Chasm challenge is not a technology issue. Organizations have dumped tens if not hundreds of millions of technology dollars into that chasm. And that's what organizations have gotten wrong—chartering the **Information Technology** (**IT**) department to cross the Analytics Chasm.

If organizations want to cross the Analytics Chasm phase to become more predictive and prescriptive in their business operations, then they need to embrace *an economics mindset, not a technology mindset*. And that requires senior management to let go of outdated legacy data and analytic beliefs.

  DEAN OF BIG DATA TIP:

Economics is a branch of knowledge concerned with the production, consumption, and distribution of wealth (or value).

An economics mindset can help organizations cross the Analytics Chasm by:

- Transforming from an IT mentality of using data and analytics to monitor the business, to a business mindset that seeks to predict what's likely to happen in order to prescribe actions to prevent or monetize that prediction.

- Moving beyond aggregating data to reduce storage and data management costs, to analyzing and mining all the detailed transactions and engagement data at the level of the individual (human or device).

- Expanding data access from a restrictive tabular data model to providing access to all data sources—internal and external, structured and unstructured—that *might* yield useful customer, product, and operational insights at the level of the individual (human or device).

- Transitioning from a batch data processing environment to an operational model that can process and analyze the data in real-time in order to catch customers or operations "in the act" to create new value creation and monetization opportunities (see *Figure 1.2*).

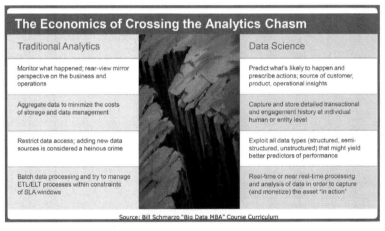

Figure 1.2: The Economics of Crossing the Analytics Chasm

Crossing the Analytics Chasm requires organizations to leverage the economics of data and analytics using a use case-by-use case approach to make the leap. We will discuss the use case-by-use case approach in more detail in *Chapter 4, University of San Francisco Economic Value of Data Research Paper*, an approach which is the key to determining and exploiting the economic value of the organization's data.

Phase 2: Business Insights: This phase seeks to **uncover** actionable customer, product, and operational insights buried within and across the organization's data. The Business Insights phase is where the organization seeks to predict "what is likely to happen next" with respect to its customers, products, and operations. The Business Insights phase *explores* a wide variety of internal and external data sources, using data engineering techniques (for example, data transformation, data enrichment, metadata enhancement, data blending) and a variety of advanced analytic techniques (predictive analytics, data mining) in an effort to uncover strategic, actionable, and material insights that *might* be useful in predicting performance.

The Business Insights phase is where the collaboration between the business stakeholders and the data science team becomes indispensable in *identifying those variables and metrics that* **might** *be better predictors of performance.*

The data science team seeks to identify and codify the customer, product and operational insights (trends, patterns, and relationships) buried in the data. These insights form the basis for transitioning to *Phase 3: Business Optimization.*

Phase 3: Business Optimization: The Business Optimization phase seeks to **embed** prescriptive analytics (recommendations and propensity scores) into the operational systems in order to automate the optimization of the organization's key operational processes. These systems seek to constantly optimize their operations based upon each customer engagement or operational interaction. In this phase, organizations seek to automate parts of their business operations with advanced analytic modules that automatically optimize operational performance. This phase leverages predictive analytics, prescriptive analytics, and supervised and unsupervised ML to create specific, operational recommendations.

 **DEAN OF BIG DATA TIP:**

Supervised Machine Learning uncovers relationships between variables buried in datasets given a known outcome or label (unknown knowns); it learns and codifies the relationships between multiple dependent variables and a known outcome variable.

Unsupervised Machine Learning uncovers relationships between variables in datasets in which there is no known outcome or label (unknown unknowns): it discovers and codifies previously unknown relationships between independent variables.

Phase 4: Insights Monetization: Organizations are realizing that the best way to monetize their data isn't to sell it, but instead to leverage the customer, product, and operational insights (propensities) that have been gathered throughout the Business Insights and Business Optimization phases to create new revenue or monetization opportunities. During the Business Insights and Business Optimization phases, organizations should be **gathering insights**—propensities, tendencies, patterns, trends, associations, relationships—about their key business and operational entities (for example, customers, doctors, teachers, technicians, stores, compressors, chillers, turbines, and motors).

DEAN OF BIG DATA TIP:

The Business Insights and Business Optimization phases are internally focused; that is, they focus on leveraging data and analytics to predict, prescribe, and optimize the organization's internal use cases. However, the customer, product, and operational insights gathered during the Business Insights and Business Optimization phases will be instrumental in the externally focused Phase 4: Insights Monetization.

Insights about the organization's key business and operational entities can be aggregated, mined, classified, and clustered to identify unmet or under-served customer, product, operational, and market needs. These aggregated insights form the basis for identifying and creating net-new monetization or revenue opportunities such as new products, new services, new channels, new audiences, new partners, new audiences, new markets, and even new consumption models.

Phase 5: Digital Transformation: The final phase of the BDBMMI has as much to do with **culture** as it does with data and analytics. The key to Digital Transformation success is to create a culture that encourages the continuous exploration, creation, sharing, reuse, and refinement of an organization's digital and human assets. As we will explore in *Chapter 8, The 8 Laws of Digital Transformation*, Digital Transformation is about creating an environment where advanced analytics such as RL and AI (which I will cover in *Chapter 6, The Economics of Artificial Intelligence*) are augmenting the capabilities of the front-line employees to explore, learn, and adapt at the point of customer engagement and operational execution.

Digital Transformation must also address the organization's compensation and **rewards structure** to incentivize the business functions to share, reuse, and refine the organization's data and analytic assets. This likely means transforming how you hire, train, promote, and manage the organization to create this sharing and continuous learning and adapting culture.

🎓 **DEAN OF BIG DATA TIP:**

💡 Digital Transformation is the creation of a continuously learning and adapting business model (AI-driven and human-empowered) that continuously seeks to identify, codify, and operationalize new, actionable customer, product, and operational insights (propensities) in order to optimize (reinvent) operational efficiency, enhance customer value creation, mitigate risk, and create new revenue opportunities.

Figure 1.3 summarizes the characteristics of each of the different phases of the BDBMMI:

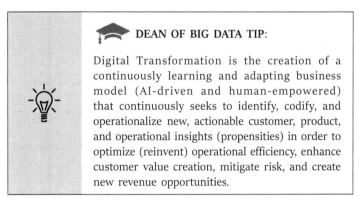

Monitoring	Insights	Optimization	Monetization	Transformation
Collect customer, product, and operational data to create retrospective reports and dashboards that monitor, report, and alert on what has happened	Apply data science and design thinking to uncover potentially valuable customer, product, and operational insights that predict business outcomes	Operationalize prescriptive analytics to optimize key business and operational processes and systems to create "intelligent" apps and "smart" products / spaces that continuously learn	Leverage customer, product, and operational insights to create new revenue opportunities (products, services, audiences, channels, markets, consumption models)	Create a collaborative / sharing value creation culture that embraces analytics as a business discipline to accelerate digital business and operational transformation

Source: Bill Schmarzo "Big Data MBA" Course Curriculum

Figure 1.3: Big Data Business Model Maturity Index Phase Characteristics

Now let's understand the action plan that organizations can follow to advance up the BDBMMI.

Navigating the Big Data Business Model Maturity Index

The problem with the BDBMMI is that the journey up the index is not a continuous process. There are different challenges that must be addressed at each phase as organizations seek to become more effective at leveraging data and analytics to power their business models. Let's review the steps required to transition between the BDBMMI phases.

Transitioning from Business Monitoring to Business Insights

Here are the actions to transition from **Phase 1: Business Monitoring** to **Phase 2: Business Insights**:

- Identify an organizational **Strategic Business Initiative**; that is, what is the organization trying to accomplish over the next 12 to 18 months from a business perspective, and what are the financial, customer, and operational impacts of that initiative.

- Identify, validate, value, and prioritize the organization's key business and operational **Decisions** that the key stakeholders need to make in support of the targeted strategic business initiative. Cluster the decisions into common subject areas or **Use Cases**.

- Capture, cleanse, normalize, transform, enrich, and make available the relevant data sources in a **Data Lake** (a data lake is a centralized data repository that allows organizations to store both structured and unstructured data at the lowest level of granularity)—at the lowest or most detailed level of **Granularity**—including historical operational and transactional data, internal unstructured data (consumer comments, technician notes, engineering specs), and external or third-party data (weather, traffic, local events, economic growth metrics, financials).

- Create an analytics (data science) **Sandbox** (data lake) that allows the data science team to rapidly ingest data (as-is; no schema required), quickly provision the necessary data engineering and data science tools. This allows the data science team to explore the data, discover patterns, trends, and relationships buried in the data, and test different combinations of data, data enrichment techniques, and analytic algorithms for their **Predictive Capabilities** in a fail fast/learn faster environment.

- Deploy and use **Predictive Analytics** to uncover potentially actionable and predictive customer, product, and operational insights (example, propensities, preferences, patterns, trends, interests, passions, affiliations, associations, and sentiments) buried in the data.

- Train business users to "Think Like A Data Scientist" to unleash the organization's tribal knowledge and brainstorm variables and metrics that *might* be better predictors of performance (see *Figure 1.4*).

- Create a "**Right time**" analytics capabilities that monitors individual and device "behaviors" to flag anomalies or behavioral changes that *might* be worthy of further analysis and action.

- Master **Data Science** capabilities including Data enrichment, Data visualization, Statistics, Diagnostic analytics, Data mining, and Predictive analytics.

- Master **Design Thinking** capabilities such as Personas (key personality and/or operating traits of a key stakeholder who is relevant to the problem at hand), Stakeholder Maps (a relationship map between stakeholders who either impact or are impacted by the problem at hand), Envisioning (a facilitated brainstorming exercise across a diverse set of stakeholders), Facilitation (a discovery and exploration process guided by a trained facilitator), Hypothesis Development (a design template that defines the criteria against which a successful data science engagement will be measured), and Illustrative Analytics (mocked up analytics designed to nurture and validate stakeholder analytic requirements).

- Develop **Business Case** with financial and business justification and supporting **Return on Investment** (**ROI**) analysis.

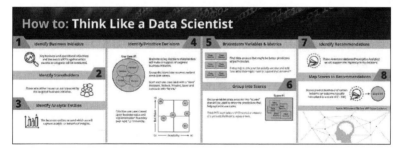

Figure 1.4: The "Think Like a Data Scientist" Methodology

Transitioning from Business Insights to Business Optimization

Here are the actions to transition from **Phase 2: Business Insights** to **Phase 3: Business Optimization**:

- Evaluate the customer, product, and operational **Analytic Insights** uncovered in the Business Insights phase for business and operational relevance based upon the **Strategic, Actionable, and Material** value of those insights with respect to the business and operational objectives of the top-priority use cases.

- Develop **Prescriptive and Preventative Analytics** (preventative analytics are analytic outcomes that provide the analytic insights necessary to prevent an action or event from happening) in order to deliver actionable recommendations and propensity scores in support of the business and operational stakeholders' key **Decisions** with respect the top-priority business and operational **Use Cases**.

- Deploy a **Data Lake** with full data management capabilities (indexing, cataloging, metadata enrichment, governance, security) that supports **Collaborative Value Creation** between business stakeholders, IT, and the data science team. The data lake must support the data science team's need for rapid data ingestion, feature engineering, data exploration and discovery, data enrichment, and analytic model development and testing.

- Capture or store the customer, product, and operational insights in **Asset Models** (**Analytic Profiles** for humans and **Digital Twins** for devices and machines) that aggregate the analytic insights about the organization's key business entities.

- Leverage **DevOps** disciplines to operationalize the customer, product, and operational insights into the organization's key operational systems. **Operationalize** the prescriptive recommendations with modern DevOps techniques to embed the analytic insights (propensities) into operational systems in an easy-to-understand, easy-to-consume format.

- Measure **Decision Effectiveness**. Instrument the analytic recommendations in order to determine the effectiveness of the recommendations. Use the results of the effectiveness measurements to refine and finetune the analytic models.

- Master **Data Science** capabilities such as feature engineering, ML, DL, reinforcement learning and AI.

- Master **Design Thinking** capabilities such as customer journey maps, mockups, prototyping, and storyboards.

- Master **Value Engineering** to quantify the economic value of data and analytics on the organization's top priority business and operational use cases (a topic that we will discuss in detail in *Chapter 2, Value Engineering: The Secret Sauce for Data Science Success*).

Transitioning from Business Optimization to Insights Monetization

Here are the actions to transition from **Phase 3: Business Optimization** to **Phase 4: Insights Monetization**:

- Aggregate, cluster, and classify the customer, product, and operational insights, captured in the Analytic Profiles, into new revenue or **Monetization** opportunities. Create a rough order estimate of market size and viability of new monetization opportunities and assess how the new opportunities leverage and/or extend existing data and analytic digital assets.

- Create customer and operational **Journey Maps** to identify sources of customer and market value creation and then map those sources of **Value Creation** against the organization's internal data and analytic capabilities for **Value Capture**.

- Explore new customer and market "as a service" consumption models that not only support the new **Monetization Opportunities** but yield new sources of customer, product, and operational insights that can be further mined to derive and drive new sources of value.

- Apply **Data Science** concepts such as Asset Models, Analytic Profiles, and Digital Twins (a digital representation of a physical asset such as a wind turbine or a compressor) to capture and fuel new sources of customer, product, and operational value.

- Apply **Design Thinking** concepts such as Personas, Prototypes, Customer Journey Maps, and Storyboarding to validate these new sources of customer, product, and operational value.

- Test, validate, and **Operationalize** the data management and data science development and production processes.

- Create a **Business Plan** that articulates and quantifies how the organization can operationalize these new monetization opportunities.

Transitioning from Insights Monetization to Digital Transformation

And finally, here are the actions to transition from **Phase 4: Insights Monetization** to **Phase 5: Digital Transformations**:

Digital Transformation is the creation of a continuously learning and adapting business model (AI-driven and human-empowered) that continuously seeks to identify, codify, and operationalize new, actionable customer, product, and operational insights (propensities) in order to optimize (reinvent) operational efficiency, enhance customer value creation, mitigate risk, and create new revenue opportunities.

- Drive business decisions by leveraging the **Economic Value of Data**. Create an operational environment that continuously seeks to capture new sources of customer, product and operational data.

- Leverage **Design Thinking** techniques to create a **Collaborative Value Creation Culture** that supports and fuels ideation and exploits innovative conflict. Force cross-organizational collaboration around purposefully constructed operational conflicts (that is, increase X while decreasing Y) to fuel envisioning, brainstorming, and organizational innovation.

- Create composable, reusable, continuously learning **Analytic Modules** that appreciate in value the more that they are used through the use of Deep Reinforcement Learning and AI (something that we will cover in *Chapter 6, The Economics of Artificial Intelligence*).

- Update the **Key Performance Indicators** (**KPIs**) and **Metrics** against which business progress and success will be measured. Understand any potential second-order ramifications from those KPIs including the costs associated with **False Positives** and **False Negatives** when making strategic business and operational decisions. Ensure **everyone** in the organization has a "clear line of sight" from their day-to-day operations and those KPIs and metrics that measure business success.

DEAN OF BIG DATA TIP:

False Positives and False Negatives are situations where the predictive models are wrong with their conclusions. Understanding and managing for the costs of False Positives and False Negatives are critical to making informed policy and operational decisions. For example with a disease:

- A False Positive is incorrectly classifying a healthy person as being infected.

- A False Negative is incorrectly classifying an infected person as being healthy.

- Create an analytics-enabled 3rd-party **Co-creation Ecosystem** that enables the organization to accelerate the capture, commercialization, and monetization of the organization's intellectual property.

- Create **Intelligent Apps**, **Smart Places,** and **Smart Things** that are continuously learning and adapting based upon every customer engagement and operational interaction.

- Create a culture that leverages Deep Reinforcement Learning and AI that **empowers front-line employees** so the organization **never misses an opportunity to learn**.

Now we want to test what we have learned about the BDBMMI with a little homework assignment.

Testing the Big Data Business Model Maturity Index

Let's say that your business initiative is to "reduce unplanned operational downtime." That's a business objective that can apply to many industries including manufacturing, entertainment, transportation, oil and gas, power, financial services, telecommunications, and healthcare. And with the bevy of IoT devices and sensors exploding on the marketplace, now would be the perfect time to address this wide-ranging, value-destroying operational problem.

Reducing unplanned operational downtime, however, is more than just an IoT challenge, because the source of much of your unplanned operational downtime may have nothing to do with machinery and device problems. Instead, it may have lots to do with those pesky human customers and their unreliable behavioral patterns. So be sure to contemplate both human and device behavioral patterns. You can use *Table 1.1* and *Figure 1.5* to help with your homework assignment.

Table 1.1 provides a checklist of the steps to navigate the Big Data Business Model Maturity Index.

Transition Phases	Transition Phase Characteristics
Crossing the Analytics Chasm from Business Monitoring to Business Insights	• Identify, validate, value, and prioritize the use cases that comprise the "unplanned operational downtime" business initiative including **use cases dependencies**. Supporting use cases could include demand forecasting, maintenance scheduling, inventory availability, consumables management, appropriate staffing, tools and equipment availability, and events impact. • Gather **potentially interesting** data sources that support your top priority use cases into the data lake at the lowest level of granularity. Data sources could include sensor readings, maintenance notes, engineering specs, technician certifications and experience, consumer comments, inventory and consumables, local events, weather, traffic, economic variables, and so on. • Explore a wide range of **illustrative analytics** using a sub-set of operational data to identify and validate best analytics approaches. • Use statistics and predictive analytics to measure **cause-and-effect** and codify patterns, trends, relationships, and associations buried within and across the datasets. • Start exploring simple analytic models to **predict** product, device, and human behaviors that are indicative of potential operational problems.

From Business Insights to Business Optimization	• Continue to **test, learn, and refine** your predictive models until you reach the required model accuracy level and "Goodness of Model Fit" as defined by the costs of False Positives and False Negatives.
	• **Repeat** until model accuracy and goodness of fit meet the use case requirements. Note: you can avoid overfitting of your models by ensuring that you have defined a robust set of metrics against which to measure model performance.
	• Create **prescriptive and preventative analytics** that deliver maintenance, inventory, staffing, and customer recommendations that prevent operational downtime problems.
	• Capture customer, product, and operational insights (propensities) within the **Asset Models** (Digital Twins for devices, Analytic Profiles for humans) that reside in the Data Lake.
	• **Operationalize** the prescriptive and preventative analytics by coming full circle to integrate the analytic outputs and results into the operational systems.
	• Instrument the **analytic results** to capture and measure the effectiveness of the prescriptive recommendations delivered by the analytic models.
From Business Optimization to Insights Monetization	• Enhance and enrich **Asset Models** (Digital Twins for devices, Analytic Profiles for technicians, engineers, and customers) with propensity scores, and strength and direction of relationships and associations (using graph analytics).
	• Leverage **Asset Models** to mine, discover, aggregate, and validate unmet or underserved customer, product, operational, or market needs.
	• **Operationalize** unmet or underserved customer, product, operational, or market needs to create new monetization opportunities via new products, services, markets, channels, audiences, partners, and consumption models.

From Insights Monetization to Digital Transformation	• Leverage **Digital Assets** (data and customer, product, and operational insights) to reinvent the organization's business models to continuously capture and exploit new sources of customer and market value creation.
	• Create composable, reusable, continuously learning **Analytic Modules** that appreciate in value the more that they are used through the use of Deep Reinforcement Learning and AI (something that we will cover in *Chapter 6, The Economics of Artificial Intelligence*).
	• Change KPIs and **Metrics** against which the organization measures business and operational progress and success.
	• Change hiring, management, and promotion models to create a **Culture of Collaboration** and **Innovative Exploration**.
	• Change the **Compensation** system to create a culture that rewards sharing and collaboration that proactively seeks to identify and eliminate business, operational, and organizational silos.
	• Create a culture that leverages Deep Reinforcement Learning and AI that **empowers front-line employees** so the organization **never misses an opportunity to learn**.
	• Apply **Artificial Intelligence** to create a continuously learning and adapting (autonomous) business model that continuously seeks to identify, codify, and operationalize new actionable customer, product, and operational insights (propensities) in order to optimize (reinvent) operational efficiency, enhance customer value creation, mitigate risk, and create new revenue opportunities.

Table 1.1: Checklist of BDBMMI Transition Steps

Figure 1.5 summarizes the Big Data Business Model Maturity Roadmap.

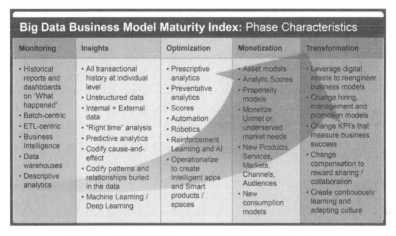

Big Data Business Model Maturity Index: Phase Characteristics				
Monitoring	**Insights**	**Optimization**	**Monetization**	**Transformation**
• Historical reports and dashboards on "What happened" • Batch-centric • ETL-centric • Business Intelligence • Data warehouses • Descriptive analytics	• All transactional history at individual level • Unstructured data • Internal + External data • "Right time" analysis • Predictive analytics • Codify cause-and-effect • Codify patterns and relationships buried in the data • Machine Learning / Deep Learning	• Prescriptive analytics • Preventative analytics • Scores • Automation • Robotics • Reinforcement Learning and AI • Operationalize to create Intelligent apps and Smart products / spaces	• Asset models • Analytic Scores • Propensity models • Monetize Unmet or underserved market needs • New Products, Services, Markets, Channels, Audiences • New consumption models	• Leverage digital assets to reengineer business models • Change hiring, management and promotion models • Change KPI's that measure business success • Change compensation to reward sharing / collaboration • Create continuously learning and adapting culture

Figure 1.5: Big Data Business Model Maturity Index Roadmap

Summary

Chapter 1, The CEO Mandate: Become Value-driven, Not Data-driven, sets the stage for the rest of the book. If organizations are ready to embrace that "data is the new oil" and the catalyst for the economic growth of the 21st century—then addressing this question becomes paramount to the organization's digital transformation success:

How effective is our organization at leveraging data and analytics to power our business models?

The BDBMMI provides a benchmark against which organizations can compare themselves. But equally important, the Big Data Business Maturity Model provides a roadmap or a guide. It guides organizations in transitioning from retrospective reports that tell them what happened, towards predictions as to what is likely to happen, and prescriptive, and preventative actions based upon those predictions. It guides organizations in helping to monetize their customer, product and operational insights, and finally towards digital transformation.

Crossing this Analytics Chasm is not a technology challenge; it's an economic challenge for how organizations leverage the economic value of data to derive and drive new sources of customer, product, and operational value.

Further Reading

1. *"The world's most valuable resource is no longer oil, but data," Regulating the internet giants, The Economist,* May 6, 2017: `https://www.economist.com/leaders/2017/05/06/the-worlds-most-valuable-resource-is-no-longer-oil-but-data`

Homework

1. Where on the BDBMMI does your organization sit vis-à-vis best-in-industry usage of data and analytics?

Stuck in Report Generation Hell - Phase 1	Some functions have advanced to Phases 2 & 3	Monetizing customer, product, operational insights	Continuously learning, adapting business model

1	2	3	4	5	6	7	8	9	10

Score:_____ Assessment: _____

_____

_____

2. How committed is business leadership to leveraging data and analytics to power the business?

Little interest from Exec Management	Have pilots with Exec sponsorship	Some success exploiting the economics of data	Business mandate to exploit the economics of data

1	2	3	4	5	6	7	8	9	10

Score:_____ Assessment: _____

_____

_____

_____

3. How well is the culture of your organization prepared to navigate the BDBMMI?

Weak culture of cross-functional collaboration	Pockets of collaboration and sharing insights	Collaboration and sharing insights the norm	Embrace conflict to fuel transformation

1	2	3	4	5	6	7	8	9	10

Score:_____ Assessment: _____

_____

_____

_____

4. What business initiative do you think could benefit the most from a tighter integration of data and analytics? What specifically could analytics do to power that initiative?

_____

_____

_____

_____

2

VALUE ENGINEERING: THE SECRET SAUCE FOR DATA SCIENCE SUCCESS

If we believe that the Big Data Business Model Maturity Index described in *Chapter 1, The CEO Mandate: Become Value-driven, Not Data-driven*, is **what** organizations could do to become more effective at leveraging data and analytics to power their business models, then your next question is "**How** can I achieve that?"

Let me introduce you to the Data Science Value Engineering Framework (see Figure 2.1).

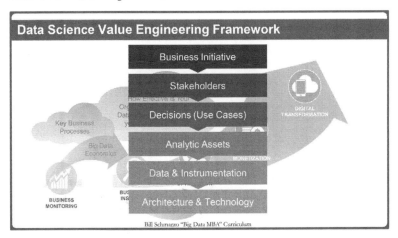

Figure 2.1: Data Science Value Engineering Framework

The Data Science Value Engineering Framework (process) provides a simple yet effective methodology for exploiting the economic value of your data and analytic assets; a methodology to drive the collaboration between the business subject matter experts (stakeholders) and your data science team to apply data and analytics to improve the operational and business effectiveness of all industries including healthcare, public safety, manufacturing, transportation, energy, education, the environment, sports, entertainment, financial services, retail, and more.

Let's drill into each of the steps of the Data Science Value Engineering Framework—the "**How** to do it" framework.

Step 1: Identify a Strategic Business Initiative

If we are focused on using Value Engineering to deliver meaningful and relevant value, then the **How** conversation must start with a focus on a business' **Strategic Business Initiatives**. A strategic business initiative is characterized as:

- Critical to immediate-term business success.

- Documented (either internally or publicly).

- Cross-functional (involves more than one business function).

- Owned and/or championed by a senior business executive.

- Has an actionable and measurable financial goal (that is, reduce, increase, optimize, rationalize).

- Has a defined delivery timeframe (12 to 18 months).

An organization's key business initiatives can be found in annual reports, analyst briefings, executive conference presentations, press releases, or a chat with your executives.

Moving your data center to the cloud, transitioning from Skype to Zoom, and arming your employees with tablet computers... are *not* strategic business initiatives. Those are technology initiatives that may or may not have defensible, financially measurable, business or operational impact.

 DEAN OF BIG DATA TIP:

Examples of **key business initiatives**:

- Reduce inventory costs
- Reduce unplanned operational downtime
- Improve customer retention
- Improve yield
- Improve technician "first time fix" effectiveness
- Improve supply chain reliability and quality

Strategic business initiatives focus on **business outcomes** that have articulated **financial value** such as optimizing operational efficiency, reducing costs, improving revenues and profits, enhancing customer value creation, mitigating risk, and creating new revenue opportunities.

Step 1A: Identify Metrics against which to Measure Progress and Success

A critical part of understanding your strategic business initiative is to identify the **metrics** and **Key Performance Indicators** (**KPIs**) against which the success or progress of that business initiative will be measured.

For example, if our key business initiative is to increase "Same Store Sales" (where "Same Store Sales" is defined as the difference in revenue generated by an organization's existing outlets or stores over a certain period as compared to the similar previous period), the following metrics or KPIs might be critical in measuring the progress and success of that initiative: Average Revenue per Visit, Volume of Store Traffic, Revenue per Employee, Line Wait Time, % Abandonment, % Mobile Orders, Positive Social Media Mentions, and "Table Turns" (the time it takes to convert or "turn" a table from one customer to the next customer).

 DEAN OF BIG DATA TIP:

Make sure you have a robust set of metrics and KPIs to avoid the **unintended consequences** that can occur due to a too narrow view on how the organization will measure the business initiative progress and success. Brainstorm multiple **lead indicators** that can provide early readings on the progress and success of the business initiative, and then prioritize those lead indicators (because not all measures are of equal value.

Step 2: Identify Key Business Stakeholders

Once we have identified the targeted business initiative and the metrics against which we are going to measure progress and success, next we want to identify the **Business Stakeholders** who either impact or are impacted by the targeted business initiative. The stakeholders typically represent 4 to 5 different business functions in order to yield a diverse set of perspectives on how the organization plans to address the targeted business initiative.

Ideally, we want can create a **Persona** (a Design Thinking tool) for each potential stakeholder to help us better understand their individual as well as the overall organizational challenges, roles, responsibilities, pain points, and key operational decisions for the targeted business initiative (see *Figure 2.2*).

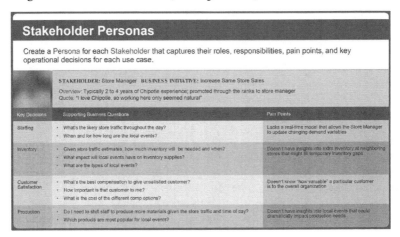

Figure 2.2: Stakeholder Personas

As you build the Stakeholders Personas, be sure to ask and understand "Why is this business initiative important to them?" and "What is their personal win condition or personal benefit from the successful execution of this business initiative?"

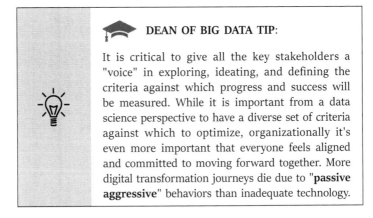

DEAN OF BIG DATA TIP:

It is critical to give all the key stakeholders a "voice" in exploring, ideating, and defining the criteria against which progress and success will be measured. While it is important from a data science perspective to have a diverse set of criteria against which to optimize, organizationally it's even more important that everyone feels aligned and committed to moving forward together. More digital transformation journeys die due to "**passive aggressive**" behaviors than inadequate technology.

Step 3: Brainstorm and Prioritize Decisions (Use Cases)

The next step in the Value Engineering process is to brainstorm the **Decisions** that each of the different stakeholders needs to make in support of the targeted business initiative. My findings are that if you identify the right set of stakeholders in *Step 2*, then the brainstorming and prioritizing of decisions flows very quickly and naturally. Why? Because these stakeholders inherently know the decisions that they have to make in support of the business initiative as they have been trying to make these decisions for year...decades...maybe even generations. Examples of such decisions include:

- Who are my most valuable customers?
- Which students are at risk of attrition?
- What products are likely to break?
- How much inventory am I going to need?
- Which marketing promotion is optimal for the target audience?
- What's the optimal price?
- What's the optimal discount to get the customer to buy?
- What are the right dietary recommendations for this individual?

My observation is that while the decisions have not changed over the years, what has changed—courtesy of massive datasets and advanced analytic algorithms like AI, Machine Learning, and Deep Learning—are the answers. And that's where the Data Scientists who are trained to optimize decisions come into play.

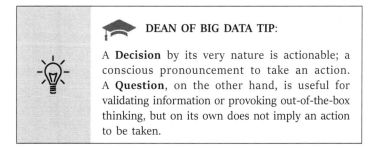

DEAN OF BIG DATA TIP:

A **Decision** by its very nature is actionable; a conscious pronouncement to take an action. A **Question**, on the other hand, is useful for validating information or provoking out-of-the-box thinking, but on its own does not imply an action to be taken.

At this stage of the Value Engineering process, we need to aggregate decisions into **Use Cases** or clusters of decisions around a common subject area that have measurable financial ramifications. To facilitate the aggregation of the decisions into use cases, we use the frame of the targeted business initiative to guide the process.

In *Figure 2.3*, the targeted business initiative is to "Increase Same Store Sales." On the left side of *Figure 2.3* are the brainstormed stakeholder decisions that support the targeted business initiative. Then we use the "Increase Same Store Sales" business initiative to group the individual decisions into clusters of decisions (use cases) around common subject areas such as increase store traffic, increase shopping bag revenue, and increase corporate catering.

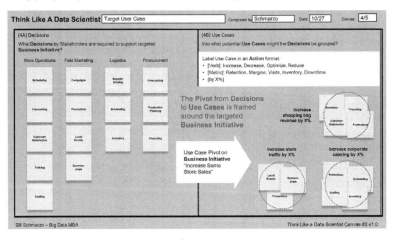

Figure 2.3: Pivoting from Decisions to Use Cases

We then label the use cases in *Figure 2.3* in an **Action Format**:

1. Identify the appropriate [**Verb**]. Example **Verbs** could include Increase, Decrease, Optimize, Reduce, Consolidate, Rationalize, and so on.

2. Identify the [**Metric**] we are looking to impact. Examples **Metrics** could include Customer Retention, Margins, Visits, Inventory, Unplanned Downtime, Fraud, Waste, Shrinkage, and so on.

3. Give the use case a [**by X%**] goal. Note: you don't need an exact goal at this time in the Value Engineering process. It is sufficient just to use the generic goal of [**by X%**].

Finally, we use the **Prioritization Matrix** to drive consensus across the different stakeholders on the top priority use cases based upon the value and implementation feasibility of each use case vis-à-vis each other over the next 9 to 12 months. The Prioritization Matrix process provides a framework for driving organizational alignment around the relative value and implementation feasibility of each of the organization's use cases (see *Figure 2.4*).

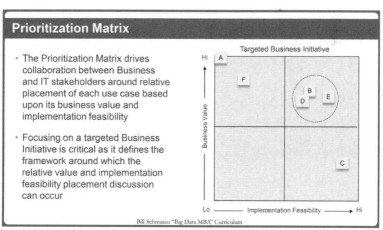

Figure 2.4: Prioritization Matrix

Some key points about the Prioritization Matrix:

- The Prioritization Matrix process weighs the "value" (financial, customer, operational, and environmental) of each use case against the implementation feasibility (data, architecture, technology, skills, timeframe, and management support) of those same use cases over the next 12 to 18 months.

- The Prioritization Matrix process gives everyone an active voice in the identification, discussion, and debate on use case value and implementation feasibility.

The Prioritization Matrix is the most powerful business alignment tool I've ever used. It works every time...if you do the proper preparation work and are willing to put yourself in harm's way as the facilitator.

 DEAN OF BIG DATA TIP:

Note: Steps 1 through 3 are covered in excruciating detail in my previous book, *The Art of Thinking Like a Data Scientist*, including templates and hands-on exercises.

After completing *Step 3*, everything else is *"easy"* because now you have a framework against which to make the analytics, data, architecture, and technology decisions.

Step 4: Identify Supporting Analytics

Now that we know our top priority use case, we want to identify the predictive and prescriptive analytics that supports the targeted use case. Sometimes it is easier to identify the supporting analytics by asking the stakeholders what **Questions** they need to answer with respect to the targeted use case.

Then we can walk the stakeholders through the "**Thinking Like a Data Scientist**" process to convert those questions into predictions and prescriptive actions (see *Figure 2.5*).

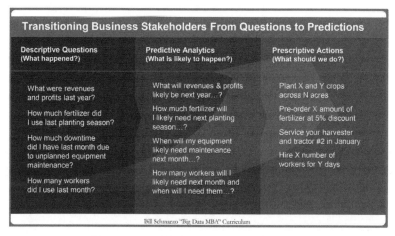

Figure 2.5: Transitioning Questions into Predictions

Figure 2.5 shows some questions and the resulting predictions and the prescriptive actions using an agricultural company example. We start with the question and then convert the question into a predictive statement, such as:

- "What were revenues and profits last year?" (the question) converts into "What will revenues and profits likely be next year?" (the prediction).

- "How much fertilizer did I use last planting season?" (the question) converts into "How much fertilizer will I likely need next planting season?" (the prediction).

Next, we ask the stakeholders if we had those predictions, how would you use those predictions to make operational decisions (which then becomes the focus of the prescriptive actions)?

It's a simple process that builds upon the questions that the stakeholders are already asking today and then guides the stakeholders to the necessary predictive and prescriptive analytics... the key to thinking like a Data Scientist.

Step 5: Identify Potential Data Sources and Instrumentation Strategy

The next step is to brainstorm with the business stakeholders what data you might need to make the predictions identified in *Step 4*. To facilitate the data sources brainstorming, we simply add the phrase "*and what data might you need to make that prediction?*" to the prediction statement.

For example:

- What will revenues and profits likely be next year...and *what data might you need to make that prediction*? The data source suggestions might include commodity price history, economic conditions, trade tariffs, fertilizer and pesticide prices, weather conditions, fuel prices, and more.

- How much fertilizer will I likely need next planting season... and *what data might you need to make that prediction*? The data source suggestions might include pesticide and herbicide usage history, weather conditions, crops to be planted, pest forecasts, soil conditions, and more.

We complete the brainstorming session between the business stakeholders and the data science team by creating a matrix of ranked data sources, using the aggregated judgement and experience of the business stakeholders, that estimates their potential predictive relevance for each Use Case (see *Figure 2.6*).

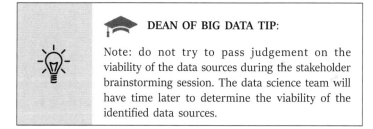

Use Cases	Increase Store Traffic Local Events	Increase Store Traffic Loyalty	Increase Shopping Bag Revenue	Increase Corporate Catering	Increase Non-corporate Catering	Improve New Product Introductions	Improve Promotional Effectiveness
Point of Sales	3	0	0	4	4	3	3
Market Baskets	2	2	3	1	3	3	3
Store Demographics	3	0	0	3	3	3	2
Local Competition	1	3	3	0	1	2	2
Store Manager Demo	1	1	2	0	2	2	1
Consumer Comments	4	0	0	3	4	4	1
Social Media	2	0	1	2	3	2	0
Weather	1	0	0	2	0	1	1
Local Events	2	2	1	1	2	1	1
Traffic	1	3	2	1	3	2	0

Data Value Assessment

Assesses the relative importance of each data source vis-à-vis its potential predictive capabilities for each Use Case

Bill Schmarzo "Big Data MBA" Curriculum

Figure 2.6: Data Value Assessment Matrix example

The data science team can then use the relative data source rankings in *Figure 2.6* to start their analytic exploration process.

> **DEAN OF BIG DATA TIP:**
>
> Note: do not try to pass judgement on the viability of the data sources during the stakeholder brainstorming session. The data science team will have time later to determine the viability of the identified data sources.

Step 6: Identify Supporting Architecture and Technologies

Finally, we'll need a modern architecture with state-of-the-art technologies (likely with lots of open source options) upon which we can build a solution that delivers the business value. While the architecture and technology choices are never easy, at least you'll understand what technologies you will need **AND** what technologies you won't need to support your targeted business initiative and the supporting use cases.

Summary

If **"what"** your organization seeks is to exploit the potential of data science to power your business models, then the Data Science Value Engineering Framework provides the **"how"** your organization can do it.

The Value Engineering Framework starts with the identification of a strategic business initiative that not only determines the sources of value but provides the framework for a laser-focus on delivering business value.

A diverse set of stakeholders is beneficial because they provide different perspectives on the key decisions upon which the data science effort seeks to optimize in support of the targeted business initiative.

The heart of the Data Science Value Engineering Framework is the collaboration with the different stakeholders to identify, validate, value, and prioritize the key decisions (use cases) that they need to make in support of the targeted business initiative.

After gaining a thorough understanding of the top priority use cases, the analytics, data, architecture, and technology decisions now have a value-centric framework within which to make those decisions (by understanding what's important AND what's not important).

Homework

1. How well do you understand the **financial impact** of the organization's **Strategic Business Initiatives**?

Don't know our strategic business initiatives		Know the financial goals of business initiatives			Know the goals & metrics for measuring success			Can personalize business initiatives	
1	2	3	4	5	6	7	8	9	10

Score:_____ Assessment: _____

_____

_____

_____

2. How well do you understand the **metrics** against which business initiative progress is measured?

Don't know the business initiative metrics		Know the business initiative metrics			Initiative metrics linked to function metrics			Initiative metrics linked to personal metrics	
1	2	3	4	5	6	7	8	9	10

Score:_____ Assessment: _____

_____

_____

_____

3. Have you aligned key **stakeholders** with the Value Engineering Framework

Limited stakeholder conversations	Created stakeholder map		Have support of all stakeholders	Have stakeholder support and budget

1	2	3	4	5	6	7	8	9	10

Score:_____ Assessment: _____

_____

_____

_____

4. Have you identified and validated **use cases** with stakeholders?

Captured some use cases from stakeholders	Captured all use cases from stakeholders	Prioritized use cases with stakeholders	Have consensus on use case financial value

1	2	3	4	5	6	7	8	9	10

Score:_____ Assessment: _____

_____

_____

_____

BILL SCHMARZO
Dean of Big Data

3

A REVIEW OF BASIC ECONOMIC CONCEPTS

The single most powerful concept in the world of business is **Economics**.

Economics is the branch of knowledge concerned with the production, consumption, and transfer of wealth or value. It is the scientific study of human action and behaviors, particularly as it relates to human choice and the utilization of scarce assets to achieve certain outcomes.

Technology is interesting and cool; it's that new shiny thing. But technology on its own is only a tool, and a tool is only as valuable as how it is used to derive and drive new sources of wealth or value.

As organizations try to determine the value of their data and analytics, they need a mechanism or framework around which to make those valuation determinations—which means understanding basic economic concepts. While some of you may have taken an economics class in college not too long ago, some more "seasoned" readers may be rusty. So, let's take the time for a quick economics refresher framed around the following question:

How effective is your organization at leveraging data and analytics to power your business model and derive and drive new sources of customer, product, and operational wealth (or value)?

Let's review some core economic concepts and consider where and how organizations can leverage these economic concepts to determine the value of their data and analytics. The economic concepts that seem to have the most bearing on determining the value of an organization's data and analytic assets are:

- Law of Supply and Demand
- Economic Multiplier Effect and Marginal Propensity to Consumer
- Marginal Costs, Marginal Revenue, and Sunk Costs
- Scarcity
- Postponement Theory
- Efficiency
- Capital
- Price Elasticity
- Economic Utility

It is my hope that this chapter fuels some creative thinking and debate as we contemplate how organizations can apply basic economic concepts to valuing these unusual data and analytic assets.

Plus, there is a bonus infographic at the end of the chapter that summarizes many of the key economic concepts covered in this chapter (that you can use and trade just like baseball cards!). But first, a little bit about the Economic Value Curve.

The Economic Value Curve

The **Economic Value Curve** measures the relationship between a dependent variable and independent variables to achieve a particular business or operational outcome, such as retaining customers, increasing operational uptime, or reducing inventory costs. The Economic Value Curve measures the impact that increasing or decreasing one of the independent variables has on the dependent variable (the business or operational outcome).

In *Figure 3.1*, for example, if we want to increase the business outcome (dependent) variable "Uptime Percentage", then we must increase our spend or investment on the "Maintenance Spend" independent variable.

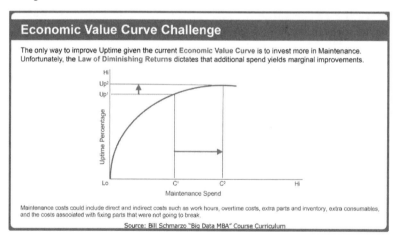

Figure 3.1: The Economic Value Curve

The challenge with the Economic Value Curve is the **Law of Diminishing Returns**. The Law of Diminishing Returns is a measure of the decrease in the marginal (incremental) output of production as the amount of a single factor of production (input) is incrementally increased, while the amounts of all other factors of production stay constant. That is, at some point, the more you spend on the independent variables, like Maintenance Spend, the less value you are getting for that spend, like Uptime Percentage.

Transforming the organization's Economic Value Curve is an area ripe for analytics-driven innovation; to leverage advanced analytics to "do more with less." We can transform the organization's Economic Value Curve by applying fine-grained predictive and prescriptive analytics to focus investments on those aspects of the independent variables that have the highest impact on the business outcomes (dependent variable).

For example, we can apply fine-grained analytics to **predict** what components are likely to fail and when they are likely to fail, and then **prescribe** the right technicians with the right experience, equip those technicians with the right parts and the right maintenance equipment, and schedule the maintenance during a planned maintenance window. By proactively taking action, the organization can improve the operational uptime business outcome while simultaneously eliminating the costs associated with unnecessary operational downtime.

In *Figure 3.2*, the impact of "do more with less" is highlighted by the green arrow where we have leveraged predictive and prescriptive analytics to transform the Economic Value Curve to increase the Uptime Percentage while decreasing Maintenance Spend.

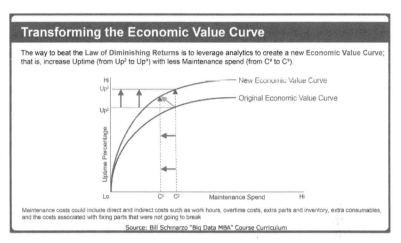

Figure 3.2: Using the Economics Value Curve to Drive Digital Transformation

Note that, *Figure 3.2* only deals with one independent variable. The interesting thing about transforming the organization's Economic Value Curve is that the more dimensions or variables against which you seek to optimize, the more creative and innovative your analytics-driven solutions must be. For example, consider the challenges of each of these scenarios:

- Increasing operational uptime while reducing maintenance costs while improving customer satisfaction, or better yet...

- Increasing operational uptime while reducing maintenance costs while improving customer satisfaction while reducing carbon footprint and emissions, or better yet...

- Increasing operational uptime while reducing maintenance costs while improving customer satisfaction while reducing carbon footprint and emissions while increasing employee job satisfaction.

The more diverse the set of variables against which the analytics need to optimize and the more granular the results, the more holistic the transformation of the organization's economic value curve. Direct marketing and loyalty card organizations have known for years the power of transforming the organization's Economic Value Curve as they applied advanced analytics using granular individually-identifiable data to drive campaign **Lift**.

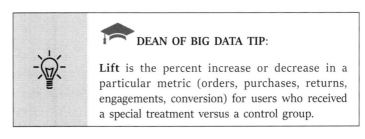

DEAN OF BIG DATA TIP:

Lift is the percent increase or decrease in a particular metric (orders, purchases, returns, engagements, conversion) for users who received a special treatment versus a control group.

Lift can be achieved when organizations have access to individually-identifiable transactional and engagement data. And as more companies are getting access to this level of detailed data (thank you, Big Data), these companies are realizing that it isn't the volume of data that one monetizes, it's the granularity at the level of the individual that one monetizes (see *Figure 3.3*).

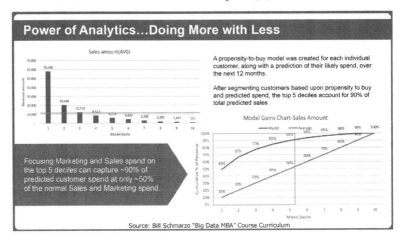

Figure 3.3: Predicting Lift to Change One's Economic Value Curve

In *Figure 3.3*, by focusing marketing and sales spend on the top 5 deciles of customers (based upon a propensity-to-buy analytic score), we can capture 90% of predicted customer spend with only 50% of the normal sales and marketing spend. That's the power of combining granular data with advanced analytics to transform one's Economic Value Curve, and that's where **Analytic Profiles** (Digital Twins for physical assets) come into play.

Analytic Profiles are an asset model for capturing analytic insights (propensities) about the organization's most valuable assets in a way that facilitates the refinement and sharing of those analytic insights across multiple use cases. An Analytic Profile consists of propensity scores, predictive indicators, clustering, segmentation, and business rules that codify the behaviors, preferences, inclinations, tendencies, interests, associations, and affiliations for the organization's key business entities, such as customers, patients, students, athletes, jet engines, cars, locomotives, CAT scanners, and wind turbines (see *Figure 3.4*).

Figure 3.4: Role of Analytic Profiles to Drive Monetization

Analytic Profiles capture detailed predictive insights for each of the organization's key business or operational entities or assets—which can be human assets or product/device assets—which facilitates the delivery of hyper-individualized, predictive customer engagement and product usage and performance recommendations. An Analytic Profile codifies the behaviors, preferences, propensities, inclinations, tendencies, interests, associations, and affiliations that can be used to predict the likelihood of a particular action for each individual customer, much like how a **Credit Score** (A credit score is a numerical expression that measures the likelihood that a particular individual will repay their loan or credit advance). Codifies and predicts an individual's likelihood to repay a loan.

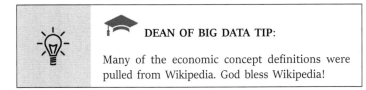

DEAN OF BIG DATA TIP:

Many of the economic concept definitions were pulled from Wikipedia. God bless Wikipedia!

Let's now review some of the more relevant economic concepts and understand their data and analytic ramifications.

The Law of Supply and Demand

The Law of Supply and Demand dictates the relationship between the quantity of a commodity that producers wish to sell at various prices and the quantity that consumers wish to buy.

Economics is governed by the **Law of Supply and Demand**, which dictates the interaction between the supply of a resource and the demand for that resource. It defines the effect that product or service availability and the demand for that product or service has on **Price**. Generally, low supply and high demand increases price, while high supply and low demand reduces the price (see *Figure 3.5*).

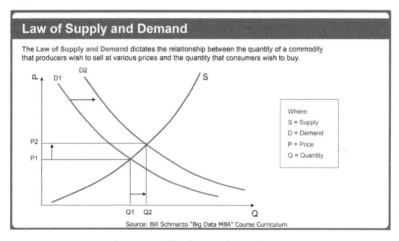

Figure 3.5: Wikipedia: Supply and Demand

Data Ramification: When we introduce the economic data valuation methodology in *Chapter 4, University of San Francisco Economic Value of Data Research Paper*, we'll quickly learn that not all data is of equal value; that the ultimate determinant of the value of a supply of data is dependent upon the demand for that data driven by its applicability and predictive relevance in helping to optimize the organization's business and operational use cases. To manage the supply and demand of data, organizations need to ask the following questions:

- What is your data supply inventory and what is the condition of that data from quality, accessibility, completeness, granularity, and latency perspectives?
- Do you have a process for identifying, validating, valuing, and prioritizing the use cases (demand) against which to apply the data (supply)?

The Economic Multiplier Effect

The Economic Multiplier Effect refers to the increase in value arising from any new injection of usage. The size of the multiplier effect depends upon **Marginal Propensity to Consume** **(MPC)**.

The **Economic Multiplier Effect** is one of the most important economic concepts developed by J.M. Keynes to explain the impact of an incremental increase in input (investment) on the resulting incremental increase in output (value). From a data and analytics perspective, the Economic Multiplier Effect manifests itself in the realization that data and analytic assets can multiple their value as they are reapplied beyond their initial use case to other use cases.

For example, when retailers installed **Point of Sale** (**POS**) systems in the early 1980s, their primary motivation was a desire to reduce labor costs while ensuring consistent pricing at the cash register. Few imagined the add-on benefits from being able to reapply the same POS dataset across numerous sales, marketing, and product development use cases, where each use case provided measurable financial value such as improving promotional effectiveness by X% or improving customer retention by X% (see *Figure 3.6*).

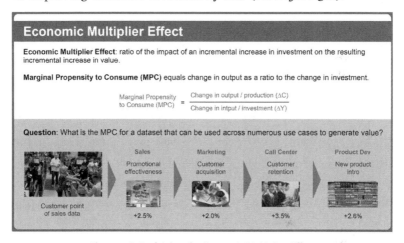

Figure 3.6: Explaining the Economic Multiplier Effect

A critical measure related to the Economic Multiplier Effect is the MPC. The MPC measures the impact of a change in output (production) as a ratio to the change in input (investment). For example, if output increases by $0.80 for each $1.00 of investment, then MPC equals 0.8 / 1 = 0.8.

Data Ramifications: If a dataset (such as POS data) can be acquired and paid for only once (investment) but can continue to generate new sources of value (production), then what is the MPC for that dataset? Of all the economic concepts, it is the Economic Multiplier Effect and the MPC that play the biggest role in helping organizations to exploit the value of their data. The ability to reuse data and analytic assets across multiple use cases at a near-zero marginal cost is truly a business game-changer. We will drill into this all-important concept in *Chapter 4, University of San Francisco Economic Value of Data Research Paper,* and *Chapter 5, The Economic Value of Data Theorems.*

Marginal Costs and Sunk Costs

Marginal Cost is the incremental change in the total cost that arises when the quantity produced is incremented by one unit; that is, it is the cost of producing one more unit of a good.

Marginal Cost is the incremental cost associated with the production of the next unit of output. Marginal costs include all the costs that vary with the level of production. Costs that do not vary with the level of production are **Fixed Costs**. Costs that vary with the level of production are **Variable Costs**. For example, the marginal cost of producing an automobile will generally include the variable costs of labor and parts needed for the production of the additional automobile but not the fixed costs of the factory that have already been incurred.

Marginal Revenue is the revenue or value gained by producing one additional unit of a good or service. An organization that is seeking to maximize its profits should produce up to the point where the marginal cost equals the marginal revenue for each additional unit of production and should stop production when the marginal costs exceed the marginal revenue (see *Figure 3.7*).

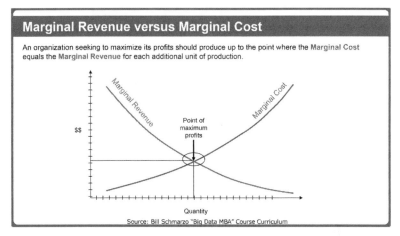

Figure 3.7: Maximizing Profits Using Marginal Revenue and Marginal Cost

When trying to master the concepts of marginal costs and marginal revenues, one must also understand the concept of **Sunk Costs**.

Sunk Costs are costs that have already been incurred and cannot be recovered.

Sunk Costs are costs already paid or incurred and for which there is no way to recover those costs; that is, the money has already been spent and you ain't getting that money back. Even though economists argue that sunk costs should not be relevant to future rational decision-making, in real life, people often weigh previous expenditures into their future decisions such as deciding to repair a car; that is, they throw good money after bad.

Through the reuse of the organization's data and analytic assets, marginal costs can be flattened (since the costs of acquiring those assets are now considered sunk costs) while marginal revenue (value) can continue to increase through the reuse of those data and analytic assets (see *Figure 3.8*).

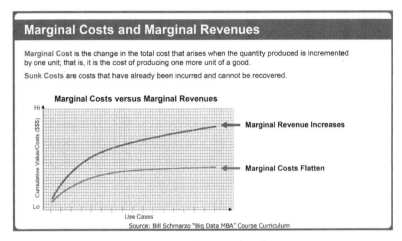

Figure 3.8: Marginal Costs and Sunk Costs

So, riddle me this Batman: What if the marginal cost of reusing an organization's most valuable asset was zero but the marginal revenue generated from the reuse of that asset was unbounded? What then would be the value of that asset?

Ah, the answer to that question is the foundation of determining the value of your organization's data and analytics, which we'll cover in detail in the next chapter.

Scarcity

Scarcity refers to limitations—insufficient resources, goods, or abilities—to achieve a desired end. Optimizing decisions about how to make the best use of scarce resources is a fundamental economics challenge.

Scarcity refers to resources being finite and limited. Scarcity means we have to decide how and what to produce from these limited resources. It means there is a constant opportunity cost involved in making economic decisions, and a need to balance unlimited needs and wants against a limited supply (see *Figure 3.9*).

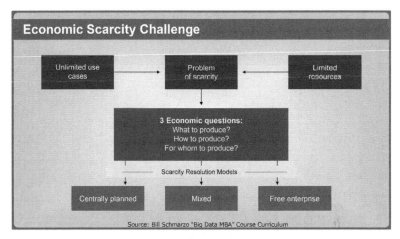

Figure 3.9: Dilemma of Scarcity

Scarcity is at the heart of the economics discussion because organizations do not have unlimited financial, human, or time resources. Consequently, organizations must master balancing their scarce assets against the nearly unlimited opportunities. And there are always more opportunities than there are resources (the real essence of the scarcity dilemma).

Data Ramifications: Scarcity plays out in the inability, or the unwillingness, of different parts of the organization to share their data and analytic assets across the organization. For some business units, their value to the organization is enhanced by the scarcity of their data; that is, whoever owns the data owns the power. This short-sighted mentality manifests itself in data silos and IT "Shadow Spend," which negates the data Economic Multiplier Effect. To overcome the data scarcity dilemma, organizations must address the following questions:

- Are your IT resources focused on capturing or acquiring the most important data in support of the organization's strategic business initiatives and the key supporting use cases?

- Are your data science resources focused on the development of the top priority, reusable analytic assets?

- Does your technical and cultural environment support—heck, even reward—the capture, refinement, and reuse of the data and analytic assets across multiple business units?

- Does your organization have an agreed upon governance methodology to manage the scarcity dilemma by prioritizing and focusing your data and analytic resources against those best use case opportunities?

Understanding the economic concepts that underpin scarcity sets the stage for understanding the data ramifications of the economic theories of postponement and efficiency.

Postponement Theory

Postponement is a decision to postpone a decision. Postponement occurs when one party seeks to either gain additional information and/or to delay the decision in search of better terms.

Postponement Theory is an economic strategy that maximizes possible benefits and minimizes risks by delaying a decision in order to gain additional data or analytic insights. That is, the decision maker believes that the benefits of delaying the decision while more data is acquired outweigh the cost of potentially making a suboptimal decision.

Data Ramifications: Postponement theory plays out when organizations decide to postpone a decision in order to gather more data and build more accurate analytics to improve the probability of making a "better" decision.

DEAN OF BIG DATA TIP:

Postponement theory is heavily influenced by the costs associated with Type I Errors (False Positive) and Type II Errors (False Negative) associated with that decision.

To make proper use of Postponement theory, organizations need to understand:

- What are the Type I Error (False Positive) and Type II Error (False Negative) risks and costs associated with the decision?

- What is the estimated effectiveness of the current decision given the Type I and Type II decision risks?

- What data *might* be needed to improve the effectiveness of that decision given the Type I and Type II errors?

- How much more accurate can the decision be made given these new data sources and additional data science time?

Efficiency

Efficiency is a relationship between ends and means. When we call a situation inefficient, we are claiming that we could achieve the desired ends with less means, or that the means employed could produce more of the ends desired.

Economic Efficiency is measured not by the relationship between the physical quantities of ends and means, but by the relationship between the value of the ends and the value of the means. When we say a process is "inefficient," we are saying that we should be able to produce the desired output with less effort or produce more output with the same effort. That's the economic equivalent of "doing more with less" that we discussed at the beginning of this chapter.

Data Ramifications: Data and analytics play a major role in driving efficiency improvements by identifying operational deficiencies and proposing recommendations (prescriptive analytics) on how to improve operational efficiencies. The aggregation of the operational insights gained from efficiency improvement might lead to new monetization opportunities by enabling the organization to aggregate usage patterns across customers segments. For example, organizations could create operational best-in-class benchmarks that could be used to measure organizational efficiencies and create goals around efficiency optimization from the aggregated performance data.

To manage the efficiency challenges, organizations must address the following data and analytic questions:

- How can we leverage our existing data to produce more output for our most important use cases?

- What other data could be acquired or gathered that could help improve operational efficiencies of our most important use cases?

- How can we leverage data and analytics to create benchmarks against which we can flag inefficient processes to help focus the organization's efficiency improvement initiatives?

Let's now explore the economic concept of **Capital** to understand its ramifications on the economics of data.

Capital

Capital is already-produced durable goods and assets, or any non-financial asset that is used in the production of goods or services.

Adam Smith defined **Capital** as "that part of a man's stock which he expects to afford him revenue." Adam Smith's definition reinforces that the ultimate economic goal of any piece of capital is to "afford (provide) revenue," which should equally apply to the organization's data and analytic assets. Capital is an input into the production function; that is, capital, including data and analytics, can be inputs into the organization's production and value creation processes.

Data Ramifications: While it may be possible to generate revenue through the direct sale of the organization's data, for most organizations, data as capital gets converted into revenue in four ways:

- Driving the on-going optimization of key operational and business use cases (for example, reducing fraud by 3% annually, increasing customer retention by 2.5% annually).

- Mitigating security, compliance, regulatory, and governance risks; avoiding security breaches, litigation, fines, theft, and so on; building customer trust while ensuring business continuity.

- Uncovering new revenue opportunities based upon superior customer, product and operational insights about unmet customer and market needs.

- Delivering a more compelling customer experience that both increases customer satisfaction and advocacy, while also increasing the effectiveness of selling and cross-selling new products and services to the highest potential customers.

Next, let's review the impact of **Price Elasticity** of demand on the economics of data.

Price Elasticity

Price Elasticity of demand is the quantitative measure of consumer behavior that indicates the quantity of demand for a product or service depending on its increase or decrease in price.

Price Elasticity of demand is the degree to which the effective demand for some item or service changes as its price changes. Price elasticity of demand is an indicator of the impact of a price change, up or down, on the demand for an item or service. As the item or service gets more expensive, fewer people or organizations can afford that item or service. Likewise, as the item or service gets less expensive, more people and organizations can consequently afford that item or service.

The price elasticity of demand is calculated as the percentage change in quantity demanded divided by the percentage change in price. If the price elasticity of demand is greater than 1.0, then the price is elastic (that is, demand for the product is sensitive to an increase in price). If the result is less than 1.0, the price is inelastic (that is, demand for the product is insensitive to an increase in price).

Data Ramifications: When considering the data ramifications from price elasticity (or the impact that changes in price have on the changes in the demand for the data), it is important to take into consideration all the costs associated with the data including:

- Data storage costs are probably the most obvious cost. As the cost of data storage continues to drop, more data should become available to more users and drive up the demand for the data.

- Analytical computing costs are also dropping. That should make more computationally intensive advanced analytics algorithms (such as Deep Learning and Reinforcement Learning) more readily available to more users.

- Data access and exploration costs are the costs associated with the user being able to access and explore the data. They are different than the storage cost and has everything to do with providing tools, training, and support for easy-to-learn, easy-to-use data access and exploration tools.

- Data confidence costs are the costs associated with instilling user confidence in the data. Data confidence costs include costs related to data accuracy, data completeness, data latency, and data governance.

Bottom-line: If your users do not have confidence in the data, then no matter how cheap the storage and computational costs, and no matter how easy-to-use the data access and exploration tools, the users just won't use the data in a way that can derive and drive value to the organization. Confidence in the data is everything, baby!

Finally, let's make sure that we understand the important role of the Economic Utility Function (because you're going to see the Utility Function concept again in *Chapter 6, The Economics of Artificial Intelligence.*

The Economic Utility Function

Utility is a term in economics that refers to the total satisfaction (or perceived value) received from the consumption or use of a good or service; the concept of utility is used to model worth or value.

Economic theories based on rational choice usually assume that consumers will strive to maximize their utility or value. The **Economic Utility** of a good or service directly influences the demand and the price of that good or service. The economic utility definition is derived from the concept of usefulness. An economic good yields utility to the extent to which it's useful for satisfying a consumer's want or need. **Marginal Utility** is the utility gained by consuming an additional unit of a good or service.

Data Ramifications: Utility is measured by the perceived value received from the consumption or use of a good or service, which means that the utility or perceived value from data and analytics is measured by the perceived value received from the consumption or usage of an additional "unit" of data and analytic assets. Much more to follow on the applicability of the Economic Utility Function in future chapters.

Summary

While the economic concepts may not apply to your daily jobs, more and more I expect that the data and analytics monetization conversations will center on basic economic concepts as organizations seek to exploit the economic value of their data and analytics to improve operational decision-making and power their business models. Data and analytics exhibit unusual behaviors from that of a traditional asset and applying economic concepts to these behaviors may help organizations as they seek to prioritize and optimize their data and analytic investments.

So, sorry for bringing back bad college memories about your economics classes, but hey, no one said that data and analytics were going to be only fun!

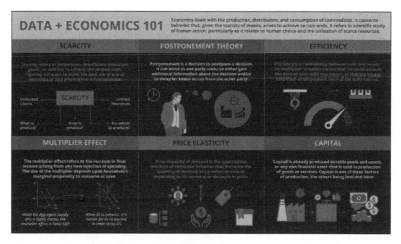

Figure 3.10: An Infographic Summary of Many of the Key Economic Concepts covered in this chapter

Further Reading

1. *Supply and Demand*: https://en.wikipedia.org/wiki/ Supply_and_demand

2. *Multiplier Effect, Macroeconomics, Akhilesh Ganti*, 17 Oct 2020,: https://www.investopedia.com/terms/m/ multipliereffect.asp

3. *Marginal cost*: https://en.wikipedia.org/wiki/ Marginal_cost

4. *Sunk Costs*: https://en.wikipedia.org/wiki/Sunk_cost

5. *Samsonike, Mans's Basic Economic Problem, Steemit*: https://steemit.com/economics/@samsonike/mans-s- basic-economic-problem

6. *The Concise Encyclopedia of Economics*, by *Paul Heyne*: https://www.econlib.org/library/Enc1/Efficiency. html

Homework

1. How often does your organization consider economic benefits as well as financial benefits?

Never discuss economic concepts	Some application of economic concepts	Growing use of economic concepts for making decisions	Embrace economics when making key decisions

1	2	3	4	5	6	7	8	9	10

Score:_____ Assessment: _____

_____

_____

_____

2. How well does your organization embrace diversity of perspective to drive a "do more with less" innovative mindset?

We avoid controversial conversations	Pockets leverage diversity to drive innovation	Execs encourage controversial conversations	Execs mandate collaboration around diverse perspectives

1	2	3	4	5	6	7	8	9	10

Score:_____ Assessment: _____

_____

_____

_____

3. How well does your organization exploit value-generating capabilities of Analytic Profiles?

Initial education on Analytic Profiles	Analytic Profile pilots underway	Some success deploying Analytic Profiles	Actively monetizing Analytic Profiles						
1	2	3	4	5	6	7	8	9	10

Score:_____ Assessment: _____

_____

_____

_____

BILL SCHMARZO
Dean of Big Data

4

University of San Francisco Economic Value of Data Research Paper

DEAN OF BIG DATA TIP:

Note: This chapter is a republishing of the original ground-breaking research paper titled "*Applying Economic Concepts to Big Data to Determine the Financial Value of the Organization's Data and Analytics and Understanding the Ramifications on the Organizations' Financial Statements and IT Operations and Business Strategies*" that Professor Mouwafac Sidaoui and I did while at the University of San Francisco School of Management.

I am including the paper in its original version (except for some minor changes) because the research process and subsequent discoveries provided the catalyst for writing this book.

This paper truly caused me to *change my frame* with respect to how I thought about determining the value of data, and ultimately, the value of analytics.

I hope you enjoy reading—and studying—it as much as I enjoyed researching and writing it!

APPLYING ECONOMIC CONCEPTS TO BIG DATA TO DETERMINE THE FINANCIAL VALUE OF THE ORGANIZATION'S DATA AND ANALYTICS, AND UNDERSTANDING THE RAMIFICATIONS ON THE ORGANIZATION'S FINANCIAL STATEMENTS AND IT OPERATIONS AND BUSINESS STRATEGIES

Abstract

Companies are contemplating the organizational and business challenges of accounting for data as a "corporate asset." Data is now seen as a currency. This research paper deep dives into the economics of data and analytics and defines these analogies.

Mr. Bill Schmarzo,
Executive Fellow, University of San Francisco School of Management

Dr. Mouwafac Sidaoui,
Associate Professor and Chair Department of Business Analytics and Information Systems

The volume, variety, and velocity of data may have changed over the past few years, but one thing hasn't changed—the value of the data to improve operational decision-making and power business strategies. This research paper will explore the following questions with respect to how organizations maximize the economic and financial value of the organization's data and analytics:

- How does an organization identify and prioritize the business use cases upon which to focus its data and analytics initiatives?

- How does an organization determine the economic value of the data that supports the organization's business use cases?

- How does an organization create a framework that facilitates the capture and reuse of the organization's data and analytic assets?

- What is the role of the data lake, data governance, data quality, and other data management disciplines in managing, protecting and enhancing the organization's data and analytic assets?

Introduction

The importance of data has changed over the years. As the volume, variety, and velocity of the data grew over the past few years, the economic value of data has been transformed by the big data phenomenon[citation 1] that has enabled organizations to capture a broader, more granular, and more real-time range of customer, product, operational, and market interactions. Today, business leaders see data as a monetization opportunity, and their organizations are embracing data and analytics as the *intellectual capital* of the modern organization.

More and more companies are also contemplating the organizational and business challenges of accounting for data as a "corporate asset."

Data as an asset exhibits unusual characteristics when compared to other balance sheet assets. Most assets depreciate with usage. However, data **appreciates** or gains more value with usage; that is, the more the organization uses the data across more use cases, the more valuable, complete, and accurate the data becomes.

However, there are severe limitations in valuing data in the traditional balance sheet framework. It is important that firms identify a way to account for their data. To address this challenge, this research paper will put forth the following:

1. A framework to facilitate the capture, refinement and sharing of the organization's data and analytic assets, and

2. A process to help organizations prioritize where to invest their precious data and analytic resources.

It is our hope that this research paper will foster new ways for organizations to rethink how they value their data and analytics from an economic and financial perspective. The concepts covered in this research paper will provide a common vocabulary and approach that enables business leaders to collaborate with the IT and Data Science teams on identifying and prioritizing the organization's investments in data and analytics; to create a common *collaborative value creation* platform.

Creating the Collaborative Value Creation Framework

Data and analytics are powerful assets in which to invest, but organizations struggle to assign these intangible assets their appropriate economic value. Assigning the appropriate value to these digital assets is important if organizations want to maximize their economic impact and optimize organizational investments in data and analytics.

Organizations need a framework—what we will call the *collaborative value creation* platform—that maximizes the economic value of data and analytic assets across the organization.

Step 1: Prioritizing Business Use Cases

To quantify the value of these intangible data and analytic assets, we need to find a basis point around which the organization can establish the *prudent value* of the data and analytics. We will use the organization's key business use cases (for example, acquiring more customers, reducing customer churn, improving the quality of care, improving customer satisfaction, reducing cybersecurity risks, reducing maintenance costs) and the financial value of these use cases to establish that *prudent value*.

Step 2: Role of Analytic Profiles

Even organizations advanced with substantial advanced analytic capabilities suffer from "orphaned analytics"[citation 2], analytics that address a one-time business need but are not "operationalized" or reused across multiple use cases. The capture, refinement, and reuse of the analytics can be addressed using a framework called an **Analytic Profile**[citation 3].

An Analytic Profile consists of metrics, predictive indicators, segments, scores, business rules, and analytic insights that provide a snapshot into the behaviors, preferences, propensities, inclinations, tendencies, interests, associations, and affiliations at the level of the individual entity such as customers, patients, students, athletes, jet engines, cars, and wind turbines.

Analytic Profiles help an organization to prioritize and align data science resources to create actionable insights that can be reused across the organization to optimize key business use cases, reduce cybersecurity risks, uncover new monetization opportunities, and provide a more compelling, more prescriptive customer and partner experience.

Step 3: Role of the Data Lake

A data lake is a data structure that holds large amounts of structured and unstructured data in its native format, that is, no schema is required to load data into the data lake. Unlike a data warehouse where the data is stored in a predefined relational structure, data in the data lake is stored as-is, in its native format. The ability to rapidly ingest, index, and catalog new data sources is critical in supporting the "fail fast / learn faster" data science efforts to identify variables and metrics that are better predictors of performance. As a result, the data lake becomes the organization's "collaborative value creation" platform by facilitating the capture, refinement and reuse of the organization's data and analytic assets across multiple business use cases.

Chipotle Use Case

We will now apply the framework and supporting process outlined in this paper to a real-world organization. We selected a public company so that we could use publicly available data to demonstrate the paper's concepts. The company that we selected was Chipotle Mexican Grill Inc.[citation 4]

Step 1: Identify a Targeted Business Initiative

A **Business Initiative** is a cross-functional plan or program that is typically 9 to 12 months in duration, with well-defined financial or business metrics. One of the business initiatives highlighted in Chipotle's 2012 annual report was increasing same-store sales.

"Last year we opened 183 restaurants, grew our revenue by 20.3% to $2.73 billion, and saw comparable restaurant sales grow 7.1% for the year. Our restaurant-level margins were among the highest in the industry at 27.1%."

This goal of increasing same-store sales by 7% will be the business initiative upon which we will apply our data valuation framework and processes.

Step 2: Estimate Financial Value of the Business Initiative

First, we need to calculate the financial value of the targeted business initiative. The process of calculating the financial value of the targeted business initiative should be a straightforward financial accounting exercise. *Table 4.1* provides an estimate of the financial value of Chipotle's *"Increase same-store sales 7%"* business initiative."

Targeted Business Initiative	
Increase Same-Store Sales by 7%	
Chipotle Sales ($000s)	$2,731,224
Number of Stores	1,410
Average Store Sales ($000s)	$1,937
7% Increase in Avg. Store Sales ($000s)	$2,073
Annual Impact ($000s)	$191,186

Table 4.1: Calculate Financial Value of Targeted Business Initiative

Step 3: Identify Supporting Business Use Cases

The next step is to identify the use cases that support the targeted "increase same-store sales" business initiative. We conduct interviews and envisioning exercises to identify the use cases across the different business stakeholders (that is, store operations, procurement, marketing, product development, finance). For Chipotle's "increase same-store sales" initiative, we identified the following use cases:

- Increase store traffic via local events marketing
- Increase store traffic via customer loyalty program

- Increase shopping bag revenue
- Increase corporate catering
- Increase non-corporate catering
- Improve promotional effectiveness
- Improve new product introductions

Step 4: Estimate Financial Value of Each Use Case

Next, we estimate the financial value of each uses case identified in *Step 3*. To estimate the financial value of each use case, each impacted business function creates a financial scenario for that use case; that is, each use case will have different financial scenarios tied to the number of business functions impacted by the targeted business initiative. For the use case "increase store traffic via local events marketing," we create three financial scenarios for the three impacted business functions of Field Marketing, Store Operations, and Product Development.

- **Field Marketing** (Scenario #1) created a scenario that estimates the incremental revenue generated from designing localized pamphlets and brochures for local events yielding a financial estimate of $62M.
- **Store Operations** (Scenario #2) created a scenario for co-branded, holiday events to be executed by local store management (Christmas event with the New York Times) yielding a financial estimate of $54M.

The business stakeholders would then collaborate to evaluate the different scenarios and select the most appropriate scenario (the scenario with a proper match of financial value and execution feasibility). The financial value of the selected scenario would then be used as the basis for the financial value of that use case. In the Chipotle "increase same-store sales via local events marketing" use case, we chose Scenario #1 (Field Marketing) with an estimated financial value of $62M.

After repeating the scenario creation, evaluation, and selection process for each use case, we end up with the following financial value for each use case (see *Table 4.2*).

Business Initiative: Increase Same-Store Sales by 7%							
(Estimated Value of Business Initiative: $191M annually)							
Use Cases							
Data Sources	Increase Store Traffic via Local Events Mktg	Increase Store Traffic via Loyalty Program	Increase Shopping Bag Revenue	Increase Corporate Catering Revenue	Increase Non-Corporate Catering Revenue	Improve New Product Intro Effectiveness	Improve Promotional Effectiveness
Financial Value ($M)	$62.0	$48.0	$26.0	$24.0	$14.0	$18.0	$27.0
Field Marketing ($M)	**$62.0**	$25.0	**$26.0**	$8.0	$10.0	$14.0	$18.0
Store Ops ($M)	$55.0	$42.0	$18.0	**$24.0**	**$14.0**	$9.0	$16.0
Product Dev ($M)	$45.0	$24.0	$12.0	$8.0	$8.0	**$18.0**	$22.0
Corp Marketing ($M)	$50.0	**$48.0**	$22.0	$10	$8.0	$12.0	**$27.0**
Procurement ($M)	$22.0	$0.0	$12.0	$0.0	$0.0	$8.0	$6.0

Table 4.2: Financial Value of Business Function Scenarios for Each Use Case

Step 5: Estimate the Value of the Supporting Data

The next step is to estimate the value of the supporting data sources. We have each business stakeholder rate the relative value of each data source with respect to each use case; that is, how important is data source #1 to use case #1, how important is data source #2 to use case #1, and so on. One can use a rating scale of 0 to 4, 0 to 10, or 0 to 100, but the finer the granularity of the data rankings, the more precise the data valuation determination.

Next, we calculate the value of each data source vis-à-vis each use case. One can make the formula as sophisticated as required, as long as the business stakeholders understand the rationale for the formula. Finally, the data source values are summed across the use cases to get an aggregated value calculation (see *Table 4.3*).

	Key Business Initiative: Increase Same-Store Sales by 7%							
	(Estimated value of Business Initiative: $191M Annually)							
	Use Cases							
Data Sources	Increase Store Traffic via local events mktg	Increase Store Traffic via Loyalty Program	Increase Shopping bag Revenue	Increase Corporate Catering Revenue	Increase Non-Corporate Catering Revenue	Improve New Product Intro Effectiveness	Improve Promotion Effectiveness	Value of Data across all use cases
Financial Value ($M)	$62.0	$48.0	$26.1	$24.0	$14.0	$17.9	$27.2	$219.2
POS Transactions ($M)	$12.4	$16.0	$6.5	$4.8	$2.8	$4.9	$6.8	$54.2
Market Baskets ($M)	$12.4	$16.0	$8.7	$4.8	$2.8	$4.9	$6.8	$56.4
Local Demographics ($M)	$9.3	$4.0	$4.3	$9.6	$5.6	$3.3	$3.4	$39.5
Traffic	$6.2	$4.0	$2.2	$2.4	$1.4	$1.6	$1.7	$19.5
Weather ($M)	$9.3	$4.0	$2.2	$2.4	$1.4	$1.6	$1.7	$22.6
Local Events ($M)	$12.4	$4.0	$2.2	$0.0	$0.0	$1.6	$6.8	$27

Table 4.3: Aggregated Financial Value of Each Data Source across All Use Cases

Step 5: Identify and Capture Analytics

The final step is to use the Analytic Profiles to identify and capture the analytics that support each use case. While the analytic results can take many forms (for example, segments, clusters, business rules, predictive indicators), we will use the analytic concept of scores as a practical way to create analytic insights.

Scores are a rating system that aids in comparisons, performance tracking, and decision-making. Scores are used to predict the likelihood of certain actions or outcomes. For example, the FICO score measures the likelihood of a borrower repaying their loan[citation 2]. Scores are actionable, analytics-based measures that support the key decisions your organization is trying to make.

Identifying and capturing the analytics is a 3-step process:

1. We first list the **decisions** needed to support the targeted use case ("Increase store traffic via local events marketing").

2. Next, we identify or brainstorm the **recommendations** that need to be developed to support the decisions. A recommendation is a suggestion or proposal, developed using prescriptive analytics, as to the best course of action.

3. Finally, we identify the **scores** and the metrics that comprise the score, that support the recommendations and decisions.

For the Chipotle "increase store traffic via local marketing events" use case, we identified three potential scores:

1. **Local Economic Potential Score**: which measures the economic potential of the area around the store.

2. **Local Vitality Score**: which measures the amount of activity or "life" around the store.

3. **Local Sourcing Potential**: which measures the feasibility of getting the necessary organic food items to support the local event marketing.

Table 4.4 brings the Decisions, Recommendations, and Scores process together.

Use Case: Increase Same-Store Sales via Local Event Marketing

Store Staffing	• How many people to staff during the local event? • What skills to staff for the store as well as promotions? • When to staff based upon the local event? • How to measure the temporary and permanent staff performance?	**Local Economic Potential Score** • Local demographics • Local economic variables • Local home values • Local unemployment rate • Number of university students **Local Vitality Score**
Store Inventory	• How much food inventory to order for the local event? • What would be the minimum quantity of each food item to reorder? • What would be the storage plan for surplus inventory?	• Miles from schools • Miles from malls • Miles from local sports venues • Local sporting events • Local entertainment events • Other local events (farmers market)
Local Events Promotions	• Which local events to sponsor? • How much marketing funds to allocate to the local event? • What types of promotions? • Special menu pricing for local events?	**Local Sourcing Potential** • Number of local suppliers • Miles from stores • Supplier production capacity • Supplier quality
Supply Chain	• Where to acquire additional inventory in case of overrun? • Who would be the vendors for reorder procurement? • How to set the quality control of the new vendors?	• Supplier reliability • Delivery feasibility

Table 4.4: Mapping Analytic Scores to Recommendations to Decisions

The end result is an Analytic Profile for each Chipotle store that captures the analytic results across all the use cases (see *Table 4.5*).

Chipotle Store 00134	NCE	Beta	Trend
Local Economic Potential Score 2.1	92	1.85	▲
Local Vitality Score 1.4	67	3.25	▼
Demographic Segments 3.2	82	2.25	▲
Behavioral Segments 3.1	65	1.90	▼
Store Traffic Score 1.0	92	2.89	▼
Store Remodel Score 1.0	55	2.75	▼
Store Loyalty Index 2.0	98	1.35	▲
Store Customer Satisfaction	88	1.74	▼
Vendor Reliability Score	99	1.10	▲
Store Employee Satisfaction Score	78	2.65	▼

Table 4.5: Chipotle Store Analytic Profile

In *Table 4.5*:

- NCE stands for Norma Curve Equivalent and is a way of standardizing scores into a 0 – 100 scale similar to a percental-rank while preserving the value equal-interval properties of a z-score

- Beta is a measure of the volatility or rapid change in the NCE score

For example, the NCE for the Store Traffic Score for Chipotle Store 00134 is very high (92 out of 100). However, the Beta or volatility of 2.89 means that the Store Traffic Score changes frequently (maybe due to being near a high school where students are only in classes during school time, or near a sporting venue which has fewer sporting events but draws large attendance for those sporting events). In this case, it would be very important for Chipotle Store 00134 to factor in the high school's class schedule or the sporting venues event schedule (and estimated event attendance) into its operational plans.

The analytic results captured in the Analytic Profile are now ready to be refined and shared across other use cases, increasing the economic value of the analytics results and addressing the "orphaned analytics" issue.

Summary

As organizations seek to leverage data and analytics to power their business models and improve operational and strategic decision-making, organizations need to manage and account for data and analytics as corporate assets. Data and analytics will become the primary economic driver in many organizations that seek to optimize key business processes, reduce security and compliance risks, uncover new monetization opportunities, and create a more compelling user experience.

Citations

1. *12 Big Data Definitions: What's Yours*: `https://www.forbes.com/sites/gilpress/2014/09/03/12-big-data-definitions-whats-yours/#45f849b413ae`

2. *How to Avoid "Orphaned Analytics*: `https://www.linkedin.com/pulse/how-avoid-orphaned-analytics-bill-schmarzo?trkInfo=VSRPsearchId%3A79026930148487352173 8%2CVSRPtargetId%3A6165930841810677760%2CVSRPcmp t%3Aprimary&trk=vsrp_influencer_content_res_name`

3. *Best Practices for Analytics Profiles*: `https://infocus.delltechnologies.com/william_schmarzo/best-practices-for-analytics-profiles/`

4. *Chipotle Mexican Grill*: `https://en.wikipedia.org/wiki/Chipotle_Mexican_Grill`

5. *Chipotle Mexican Grill 2012 Annual Report*: `https://ir.chipotle.com/annual-reports`

BILL SCHMARZO
Dean of Big Data

5

THE ECONOMIC VALUE OF DATA THEOREMS

One of the eye-opening revelations for me from the University of San Francisco Economic Value of Data research study was the differences in an accounting versus an economic asset valuation approach:

- **Accounting** uses a "Value in Exchange" methodology for determining asset valuation based upon the acquisition cost of an asset; that is, the value of an asset is determined by what someone is willing to pay you for that asset or what you paid to acquire that asset.

- **Economics** uses a "Value in Use" methodology for determining asset valuation; that is, the value of the asset is determined by how much value you can create from using that asset.

When we change our frame from an accounting to an economics perspective, understanding how to determine the value of one's data and analytic assets almost become self-evident. Once we stop trying to "force fit" data into our balance sheet, then our minds are liberated to understand the real economic potential of data—to use data and analytic assets to derive and drive new sources of customer, product, and operational value.

After releasing the University of San Francisco "Determining the Economic Value of Data" research paper, I had numerous conversations with senior executives about the business ramifications of its findings. From those conversations, I identified several "theorems" which can guide organizations in how the Economic Value of Data research could impact their organizations; what I am calling the "**Economic Value of Data (EvD) Theorems.**"

DEAN OF BIG DATA TIP:

A theorem is defined as a "general proposition, not self-evident, but proven by a chain of reasoning; a truth that is established by means of accepted truths."

EvD Theorem #1: Data, By Itself, Provides Little Value

It isn't the data itself that's valuable; it's the trends, patterns, and relationships (insights) gleaned from the data about your customers, products, and operations that are valuable.

In *Chapter 1, The CEO Mandate: Become Value-driven, Not Data-driven*, I introduced Phase 4 of the Big Data Business Model Maturity Index—the "**Insights Monetization**" phase and discussed how organizations should not focus on trying to monetize their data by *selling* it.

That's an accounting mentality. Instead, organizations should adopt an economics (**value in use**) mentality to identify opportunities to use their data to create new sources of customer, product, and operational value (see *Figure 5.1*).

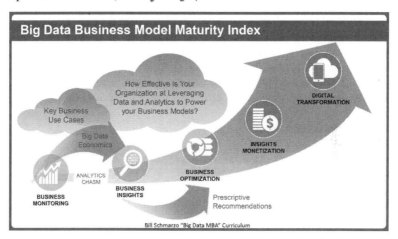

Figure 5.1: Insights Monetization Phase of Big Data Business Model Maturity Index

Many organizations are associating *data monetization* with the selling of their data. Selling data is a **business model decision**, not a business transaction. And selling data is not a trivial task, especially for organizations whose primary business is not selling data. Organizations new to selling data will need to be concerned with privacy and **Personally Identifiable Information (PII)** legislation, data quality and accuracy, data transmission reliability, pricing, packaging, marketing, sales, support, and so on. Companies such as Nielsen, Experian, and Acxiom are experts at selling data because that's their business; they have built a business model around gathering, aggregating, cleansing, aligning, anonymizing, packaging, selling, and supporting data. Plus, there are significant liabilities lurking for organizations that move into the business of selling data (in September of 2017, Equifax had a data breach that exposed the personal information of 147 million people and cost Equifax over $700M in fines and monetary relief to consumers).

Instead of trying to sell your data, organizations should focus on monetizing the customer, product, and operational **insights** that are gleaned from the data; insights that can be used to optimize key business and operational processes, reduce security and compliance risks, uncover new revenue opportunities, and create a more compelling, differentiated customer and partner engagement.

EvD Theorem #2: Predictions, Not Data, Drive Value

It is the quantification of trends, patterns, and relationships that drive predictions about what is likely to happen.

It is the quantification of trends, patterns, and relationships around customers, products, services, operations, and markets that drive operational, management, and strategic predictions. And it is the value of these predictions (in support of the top-priority business and operational use cases) that ultimately determines the economic value of your data. And the best way to codify and ultimately monetize those trends, patterns, and relationships is through the use of Analytic Profiles.

As I discussed in *Chapter 3, A Review of Basic Economic Concepts*, Analytic Profiles or Digital Twins, provide a mechanism for capturing the metrics, predictive indicators, segments, scores, and business rules that codify the behaviors, preferences, propensities, inclinations, tendencies, interests, associations, and affiliations for the organization's key business entities—whether those business entities are a human (doctor, technician, teacher, police officer, student, or patient) or a device (wind turbine, compressor, car, chiller, or locomotive). See *Figure 5.2*.

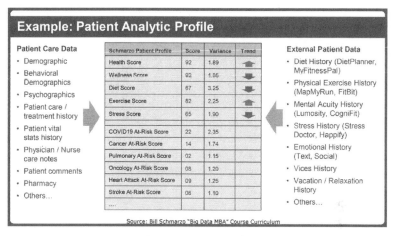

Figure 5.2: Analytic Profile

But these Analytic Profiles do more than drive the optimization of the organization's business and operational use cases. They also provide the foundation for identifying new revenue or monetization opportunities. By understanding and **predicting** your customer and product usage behaviors, tendencies, inclinations, and preferences, organizations can identify unmet customer needs or new product usage patterns that can be the basis for new services, new products, new pricing, new product bundles, new markets, new channels, new consumption models, and so on.

These **predictions**, though never 100% accurate, give organizations an "*edge*" in their operational, management, and strategic decisions. For example, having better predictions about which customers are likely to attrite and the predicted lifetime value of those customers gives you an edge in deciding upon which customers to focus (optimize) your customer retention investments. The predictions may not yield much of an edge, but sometimes it is the smallest of edges that can separate the winners from the losers.

EvD Theorem #3: Predictions Drive Value Through Use Cases

Predictions drive monetization opportunities through improved (optimized) business and operational use cases.

To fully exploit the economic value of data, the research found that a use case by use case approach enables organizations to attribute the economic value of their data based upon the reuse of that data across multiple use cases. That is, the use cases provide the linkage between the business stakeholders—who understand the financial and business value of the use cases—and the data science team—whose expertise is in identifying and codifying the variables and metrics that are better predictors of performance (see *Figure 5.3*).

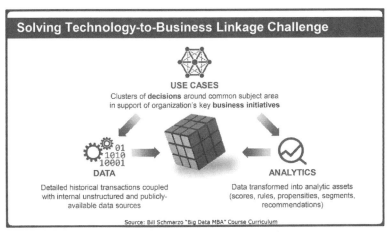

Figure 5.3: Use Cases Provide the Technology-to-Business Linkage

As an example, in Figure 5.4, the same dataset (Customer Point of Sales) can be used by Sales to increase promotional effectiveness by 2.5%, and then that same data set at a marginal cost of zero can be used by Marketing to improve customer acquisition by 2.0%, and then improve customer retention by 3.5% by the Call Center, and then improve new product introductions by 2.6% by Product Development, and so forth.

And while the financial value of 2.0% and 3.5% and so forth will vary from organization to organization, the bottom line is that there is substantial, measurable value being provided because of the re-use of that same data set across multiple use cases.

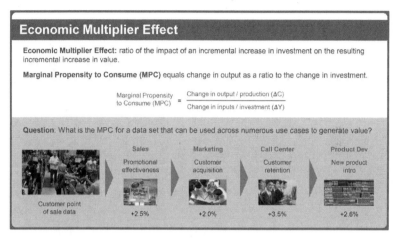

Figure 5.4: Reuse of the Data drives the Economic Multiplier Effect

This use case-by-use case valuation methodology helps organizations to determine the economic value of their data sources, which can be used to prioritize data and analytic asset investments. Since not all data sources are of equal value, the organization can consequently prioritize its data management, data governance, and date enrichment investments on those data sources that are most important to the organization.

What's most important about the Economic Multiplier Effect featured in Figure 5.4, is that the data can be reused (if in a curated format) across an unlimited number of use cases at a near-zero marginal cost. That brings us to Theorem #4.

EvD Theorem #4: The Data Economic Multiplier Effect is the Real Game-changer

The ability to reuse the same data sets across multiple use cases at near-zero marginal cost is the real economic game-changer.

The use case-by-use case approach highlighted in *EvD Theorem #3* is the key to exploiting the unique economic characteristics of data—an asset that never depletes, never wears out, and can be used across an unlimited number of use cases at near-zero marginal cost (yeah, there's the economic multiplier effect again). This use case by use case approach powers the economics "value in use" methodology for determining the value of a data set based upon the financial value of each use case (see *Figure 5.5*).

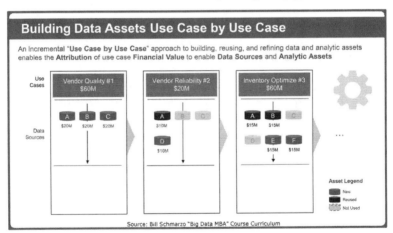

Figure 5.5: Ascertaining Data Value Use Case by Use Case

In *Figure 5.5*, Use Case #1 (Improve Vendor Product Quality) is worth $60M annually and requires 3 data sets (A, B, and C) to optimize that use case. Using a straight-line financial allocation approach, we can allocate $20M of value ($60 / 3 = $20M) to each of the 3 enabling data sets.

 DEAN OF BIG DATA TIP:

 We could use more sophisticated analytic techniques to allocate the $60M, such as Random Forest or **Principal Component Analysis (PCA)**, based upon the significance of each data set's predictive contributions. But that's a bit of overkill for right now.

Use Case #2 (Improve Vendor Delivery Reliability) is worth $20M annually and requires two data sets (A and D) to optimize that use case. We would then allocate $10M of value ($20M / 2 = $10M) to each of the 2 enabling data sets. Use Case #3 (Component Inventory Optimization) is worth $60M annually and requires four data sets (A, B, E, and F) to optimize that use case. We would then allocate $15M ($60M / 4 = $15M) to each of the enabling data sets. And so forth.

And maybe the biggest take-away from *Figure 5.5* is the ability to reuse data sets across multiple use cases at **near-zero marginal cost**. We reused data set A in Use Cases 2 and 3 at near-zero marginal cost. And we were able to reuse data set B in Use Case 3 as well. This is an important concept, into which we will deep dive in *Chapter 7, The Schmarzo Economic Digital Asset Valuation Theorem*.

The ability to easily reuse data sets is highly dependent upon the creation of a modern data lake comprised of both raw data (which the data science team plays with to determine the value of that data to improve predictive accuracy) and curated data (which is the data that has already been deemed valuable in support of a use case and has gone through the data curation processes). See *Figure 5.6*.

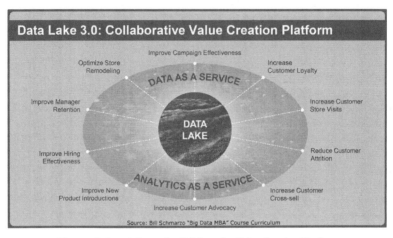

Figure 5.6: Data Lake as the Collaborative Value Creation Platform

Wikipedia says this about "data curation":

"Data curation is the organization and integration of data collected from various sources. It involves annotation, publication and presentation of the data such that the value of the data is maintained over time, and the data remains available for reuse and preservation. Data curation includes all the processes needed for principled and controlled data creation, maintenance, and management, together with the capacity to add value to data."

When the data lake is built in this iterative fashion (which also means the death of "big bang" data and analytics projects), where the inclusion of a new data source is driven by its relevance in supporting the predictive requirements of a business or operational use case, then the organization is beginning to transform the data lake into a **"collaborative value creation platform**." The "collaborative value creation platform" drives organization alignment around identifying and prioritizing the data sources that power the use case roadmap.

EvD Theorem #5: Predictions Enable "Do More with Less"

Trying to optimize across a diverse set of objectives can yield more granular, higher fidelity business and operational outcomes that enable "doing more with less."

As we discussed in *Chapter 3, A Review of Basic Economic Concepts*, the challenge with the **Economic Value Curve** is the **Law of Diminishing Returns**. The Law of Diminishing Returns is a measure of the decrease in the marginal (incremental) output of a production process as the amount of a single factor of production is incrementally increased, while the amounts of all other factors of production stay constant. We can transform the organization's Economic Value Curve by applying fine-grained predictive and prescriptive analytics in order to focus investments on those aspects of the independent variables that have the highest impact on the business outcomes (dependent variables).

This enables the organization to "**do more with less**" and overcome the Law of Diminishing Returns (see *Figure 5.7*).

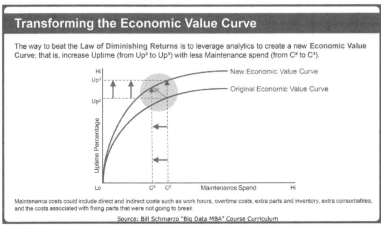

Figure 5.7: Leveraging Granular Predictive Analytics to "Do More with Less"

Also, the more dimensions against which you are trying to predict, prescribe, and optimize, the more value the organization can unleash and fulfill the promise of EvD Theorem #5: "Do more with less." Review the Economic Value Curve in *Chapter 3, A Review of Basic Economic Concepts*, for a refresher on the "do more with less" economic challenge.

The Economic Value of Data Calculation

We will end this chapter with the mathematical formula for the Economic Value of Data calculation. If you can't put the formula into math, well, it'll be hard to lay claim to that Nobel Prize in Economics that I so badly desire!

The **Economic Value of a Dataset** (*EvD*) equals the sum of the **Attributed Financial Value** (*FV*) of a specific **Use Case** (*Use_case_FV*) that each dataset provides to that specific **Use Case**:

$$EvD_{ji} = a_0 + \sum_{j=1}^{m} \left(Use\_case\_FV_j \times \frac{1}{\sum_{i=1}^{n_j} (Count\, Data\_Set_{ji})} \right)$$

where m is the number of use cases, n_j is the number of data sets per use case j, and a_o is a bias.

Using *Figure 5.5* (repeated below as *Figure 5.8* for simplicity), you apply this formula as such:

- The first iteration covers the Vendor Quality use case [*Use_ case_FV$_1$*], where [*Use_case_FV$_1$*] equals $60M. [*Count Data_ Set*] = 3 since there are 3 data sources (data sources A, B, and C) that support the analytics for [*Use_case_FV$_1$*]. Each of the 3 data sources is attributed (1 ÷ [*Count Data_Set*]) of the [*Use_case_FV$_1$*] value, which is 1 ÷ 3 or 33% of the [*Use_case_FV$_1$*] $60M value, or $20M attributed to each of the 3 data sources.

- The second iteration covers the Vendor Reliability use case [*Use_case_FV$_2$*], where [*Use_case_FV$_2$*] equals $20M. [*Count Data_Set*] = 2 since there are 2 data sources (data sources A and D) that support the analytics for [*Use_case_FV$_2$*]. Each of the 2 data sources is attributed (1 ÷ [*Count Data_Set*]), which is 1 ÷ 2 or 50% of the [*Use_case_FV$_2$*] $20M value, or $10M attributed to each of the 2 data sources.

- However, since data source A was also attributed $20M of value from [*Use_case_FV$_1$*] and $10M of value from [*Use_ case_FV$_2$*], the accumulative value of data source A is now $30M.

- And so forth, from use case to use case in attributing the value of each of the use cases to the supporting data sources.

In *Chapter 7, The Schmarzo Economic Digital Asset Valuation Theorem*, I will extend the example to include the attribution of value to the analytic assets... and more!

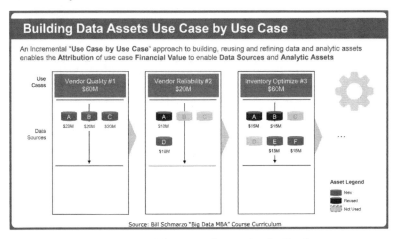

Figure 5.8: Ascertaining Data Value Use Case by Use Case

Summary

I fully expect the number of theorems to grow as the Economic Value of Data concepts mature, especially as organizations expand their value creation expectations for data and analytic assets to fuel the organization's digital transformation. For example, I can see another theorem on "variable predictability" and its importance in attributing financial value to the appropriate data sources. I guess that one will have to wait until my next research project!

We will continue to explore, learn, and share as we seek to perfect the Economic Value of Data methodology that can guide organizations along their digital transformation journey through optimizing their data, analytics, and technology investments.

Further Reading

1. *Data Curation*: https://en.wikipedia.org/wiki/Data_
    curation

Homework

EvD Theorem #1: Data, By Itself, Provides Little Value. It isn't the data itself that's valuable; it's the trends, patterns, and relationships (insights) gleaned from the data about your customers, products, and operations that are valuable.

Don't even know what data we have	Inventoried data but no method for determining value	Have identified, valued, and prioritized use cases	Have linked data sources to financial value of use cases						
1	2	3	4	5	6	7	8	9	10

Score:_____ Assessment: _____

_____

_____

_____

EvD Theorem #2: Predictions, Not Data, Drive Value. It is the quantification of trends, patterns, and relationships that drive predictions about what is likely to happen.

Basic experience in predictive analytics	Have identified top priority use case predictions	Have built top-priority use case predictions	Capturing predictions (propensities) in analytic profiles						
1	2	3	4	5	6	7	8	9	10

Score:_____ Assessment: _____

_____

_____

EvD Theorem #3: Predictions Drive Value Through Use Cases. Predictions drive monetization opportunities through improved (optimized) business and operational use cases.

No organizational alignment on approach	Single business function use case deployment	Cross-functional use case deployment	Budgeted organization-wide use case roadmap						
1	2	3	4	5	6	7	8	9	10

Score:_____ Assessment: _____

_____

_____

EvD Theorem #4: The Data Multiplier Effect is the Real Game-changer. The ability to reuse the same data sets across multiple use cases is the real economic game-changer.

Departmental data strategies and repositories	Single curated, governed data lake	Data monetization method integrated with data lake	Governance Council to prioritize use case data investments

1	2	3	4	5	6	7	8	9	10

Score:_____ Assessment: _____

_____

_____

_____

EvD Theorem #5: Predictions Enable "Do More with Less." Trying to optimize across a diverse set of objectives can yield more granular, higher fidelity outcomes that enable "doing more with less"

Settle for "Least-worst" options	Embrace diverse views in decision making	Actively embrace diverse views in decision making	Innovative methods to synergize to the "Best of the Best" options

1	2	3	4	5	6	7	8	9	10

Score:_____ Assessment: _____

_____

_____

_____

BILL SCHMARZO
Dean of Big Data

6

THE ECONOMICS OF ARTIFICIAL INTELLIGENCE

So, let me give you the key take-away lesson from this chapter right off the bat:

Using **Artificial Intelligence** (**AI**), you can create assets that appreciate in value (not depreciate), the more that these assets are used.

In this chapter, I will provide commercial proof points to that opening statement by examining Google's open-source strategy for accelerating the capabilities of the TensorFlow AI/**Machine Learning** (**ML**) framework, as well as Elon Musk's Tesla **Fully Self-Driving** (**FSD**) autonomous AI strategy for creating assets that appreciate in value through usage.

Yes, be prepared. If you're still struggling to grasp the unique economic potential of data assets—assets that never deplete, never wear out, and can be used across an unlimited number of use cases at close to zero marginal cost—then this chapter is going to blow your mind!

Let's start this exploration by revisiting a topic that was raised (and basically ignored) in *Chapter 4, University of San Francisco Economic Value of Data Research Paper*: **Orphaned Analytics**.

Orphaned Analytics

One of the most significant impediments to realizing the economic value of one's data that was identified in the Economic Value of Data research was "orphaned analytics." Now to be honest, when this issue first surfaced in the research, I really didn't give it much thought. But, as I talked to more and more clients after the release of the research paper, I started to not only appreciate the challenge of orphaned analytics but more importantly, the game-changing economic potential of transitioning the organization from a single-use, one-off "orphaned analytics" model to a composable, reusable, continuously learning analytics model that appreciates in value the more that it is used.

Orphaned analytics are one-off analytics developed to address a specific business need but never "operationalized" or packaged for reuse across the organization. Surprisingly, our University of San Francisco research on the Economic Value of Data found that this problem mostly existed in analytics-mature organizations. We found that these organizations had the deep analytics experience and staff, which made it easier to build the analytics from scratch than go through the process of searching for, finding, understanding, evaluating, and tailoring pre-existing analytics for the unique requirements of each particular use case.

These companies had such deep pools of data science and analytics talent, that it was just easier to create analytics from scratch than try to reuse something that someone else created (and probably didn't document, package, or generalize for the purposes of reuse anyway).

So, why should organizations address the orphaned analytics problem and transition to composable, reusable, continuously-learning analytic models whose value increases through usage? And how do organizations go about making that transition?

It begins with building the right **Analytics Module** architecture.

Role of Analytic Modules

The **orphaned analytics** problem can be summarized as this:

"Organizations lack an overarching framework to ensure that the resulting analytics and associated organizational intellectual capital can be captured and reused across multiple use cases. Without this over-arching analytics framework, organizations end up playing a game of analytics "whack-a-mole" where the analytics team focuses their precious and valuable resources on those immediate (urgent) problems, short-changing the larger, more strategic analytic opportunities."

Organizations' use of orphaned analytics results in the following:

- Inefficient use of data engineering and data science resources.

- Analytics projects unattached to high-level strategic initiatives.

- Limited organizational learning opportunities.

- Difficulty in gaining strategic buy-in for investments in analytic technologies, resources, and skillsets.

- Difficulty for the Data Science team when building a track record and credibility as trusted business advisors.

- Data science is never treated like a discipline, as there are no repeatable processes developed to reuse the analytics to make future (and previous) use cases continuously more efficient.

The modern organization needs an overarching analytic module framework to help organizations to capture, share, reuse, and refine the organization's analytic **Intellectual Property** (**IP**). For organizations to succeed in the 21st century, they must invest the data science and engineering time and discipline to master the development of composable, reusable, continuously learning analytic modules.

Analytic modules are composable, reusable, continuously learning analytic assets that deliver pre-defined business or operational outcomes. They are built on a layer of technology abstraction that enables the orchestration and optimization of the underlying AI/ML frameworks. Analytic modules address granular, pre-defined business problems such as anomaly detection, customer propensity to buy, an asset's remaining useful life, customer retention at-risk, predictive maintenance, operator skill evaluation, and scheduling optimization (see *Figure 6.1*).

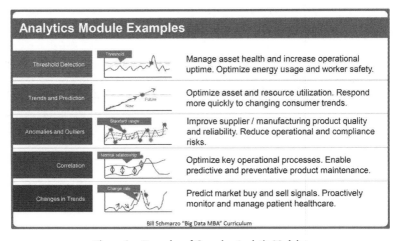

Figure 6.1: Examples of Granular Analytic Modules

One can almost think of these analytic modules as LEGO™ blocks that can be cobbled together to address bigger business problems like inventory optimization, reducing unplanned operational downtime, optimizing marketing campaign performance, and improving customer retention (though you might need some Play-Doh™ to actually link the analytic modules together).

Composable, Reusable, Continuously Learning Analytic Module Architecture

Figure 6.2 shows a state-of-the-art (as of 2020) analytic module architecture. The architecture is comprised of numerous open source components (MLflow, Seldon Core, Jupyter Notebook, Python, Spark ML, TensorFlow, and so on) built upon a Kubernetes and Docker foundation to facilitate the reuse and portability of the analytic modules across cloud hyperscalers (Amazon Web Services, Google Cloud Platform, Microsoft Azure) as well as on-premises and within embedded product environments.

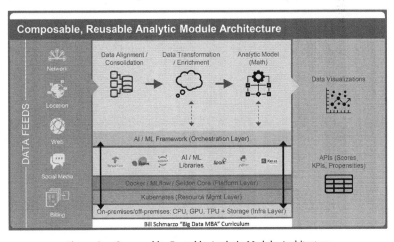

Figure 6.2: Composable, Reusable Analytic Module Architecture

These composable, reusable, continuously learning analytic modules have the following capabilities:

- Pre-defined data input definitions and data dictionary (so it knows what type of data it is ingesting, regardless of the origin of the source system)

- Pre-defined data integration and data transformation algorithms to cleanse, align, and normalize the data

- Pre-defined data enrichment algorithms to create higher-order metrics (for example, reach, frequency, recency, indices, share) necessitated by the analytic model

- Algorithmic models (built using advanced analytics such as AI, ML, and **Deep Learning (DL)**) that take the transformed and enriched data, run the algorithmic model, and generate the desired analytic outputs

- A layer of abstraction above the AI, ML, and DL frameworks that allows application developers to use their preferred or company-mandated standards

- Orchestration capability to "call" the most appropriate ML or DL framework based upon the type of problem being addressed

- Pre-defined outputs (APIs) that feed the analytic results to the downstream operational systems (for example, manufacturing, procurement, logistics, sales, marketing, web services, mobile apps)

 DEAN OF BIG DATA TIP:

 Figure 6.2 contains several open source technologies which will undoubtedly evolve over time and for which new open source technologies will emerge. Their definition as "state-of-the-art" is influenced by the technological landscape when I wrote this book in 2020.

From my experience using this analytics module architecture, I see significant improvements in not only Data Science team productivity, but as we will discuss later in the chapter, increases in the effectiveness and reliability of the composable, reusable, continuously learning analytic modules as well (see *Figure 6.3*).

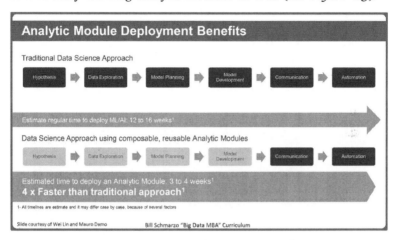

Figure 6.3: Analytic Module Deployment Benefits

In summary, analytic modules produce pre-defined analytic outcomes, while providing a layer of abstraction that enables the orchestration and optimization of the underlying ML and DL frameworks. Composable, reusable analytic modules can be created for the most common analytic needs (for example, anomaly detection, remaining useful life, operator effectiveness, likelihood to recommend, predictive customer lifetime value) and can then be linked together using technologies such as Docker containers and Kubernetes to address higher-value business and operational use cases. These could include reducing operational downtime, improving on-time delivery, reducing obsolete and excessive inventory, improving customer retention, and reducing unplanned hospital readmissions.

Before we can jump into the Google TensorFlow and Tesla FSD use cases, we might need a quick primer on artificial intelligence, DL (neural networks), and **Reinforcement Learning (RL)**.

A Quick Primer on Deep Learning, Reinforcement Learning, and Artificial Intelligence

 DEAN OF BIG DATA TIP:

While it is unlikely that you will ever be asked to build your own neural network or RL algorithm, it is important to understand how these advanced analytics work (at a high level) and what can be done with them from a value creation perspective. These are the tools of a modern-day value creation alchemist.

DL is a set of algorithms that analyze massive datasets using a multi-layered neural network structure, where each layer is comprised of numerous nodes, to train and learn to recognize and codify patterns, trends, and relationships buried in the data... without human intervention. Common applications of DL include image recognition, natural language processing, disease detection, and facial recognition (see *Figure 6.4*).

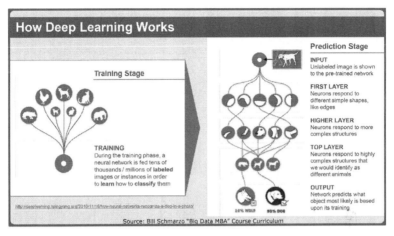

Figure 6.4: How Deep Learning Works

There are two key capabilities that underpin the continuous learning nature of DL:

- **Backpropagation** (backward propagation) improves the accuracy of neural network predictions by gradually adjusting the weights of the neural network nodes and layers until the expected model results match the actual model results. Backpropagation solves the problem of finding the best weights to deliver the best expected results.

- **Stochastic Gradient Descent** is an optimization algorithm (think second derivative in calculus) used to minimize the cost function by iteratively moving in the direction of steepest descent as defined by the negative of the gradient (slope).

Gradient descent guides the updates being made to the weights of our neural network model by pushing the errors from the model's results back into the weights (see *Figure 6.5*):

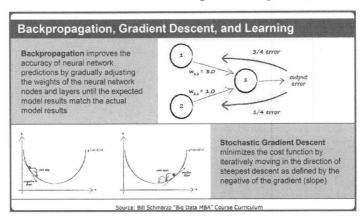

Figure 6.5: Backpropagation, Stochastic Gradient Descent, and Deep Learning

Reinforcement Learning is a type of ML algorithm that seeks to "learn" by taking actions within a controlled environment with the goal of maximizing rewards while minimizing costs. RL uses trial-and-error techniques to map situations to actions to do so.

RL is for situations where you don't have data sets with explicit known outcomes, but you do have a way of measuring whether you are getting closer to your goal (reward function). Actions may affect immediate rewards but may also affect subsequent or longer-term rewards, so the full extent of rewards must be considered when evaluating the RL effectiveness (that is, in an autonomous vehicle, the reward system must balance the short-term rewards like optimizing fuel consumption while driving a car against the long-term rewards of getting to your destination on time and safely).

RL learns by replaying a certain situation (like playing a video game or simulator, vacuuming the house, and driving a car) millions of times.

The program is rewarded when it makes a good decision and punished when it loses or makes a bad decision. This system of rewards and punishments strengthens the mapping connections to eventually make the "right" moves without programmers explicitly programming the rules into the game (see *Figure 6.6*).

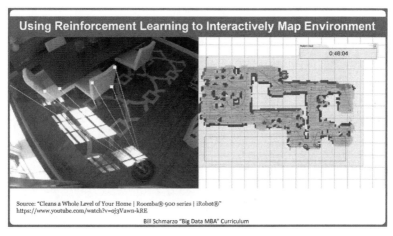

Figure 6.6: How Roomba® 900 uses Reinforcement Learning to Interactively Navigate its Environment

RL is basically playing the children's game of "Hotter or Colder." Rather than getting a specific "right or wrong" answer with each action, the system gets feedback on whether the action is heading in the right direction based upon the feedback of rewards and punishments (except I don't remember punishment being part of "Hotter or Colder").

Transfer Learning (TL) is a technique whereby one neural network is first trained on one type of problem and then reapplied to another, similar problem with only minimal training. That is, the "learning" of the neural network (the neuron weights and biases) for one use case is "transferred" to another use case.

TL is an ML approach that seeks to reuse the neural network knowledge (weights and biases) gained while addressing one use case, and apply it to a different but related use case. For example, knowledge gained while learning to recognize cars could be applied while trying to recognize trucks.

TL is key to accelerating neural network model reuse and to accelerating time-to-value and de-risking future projects through the reuse of a bona fide, real-world, working neural network model.

Artificial Intelligence is the simulation of human intelligence using advanced analytic techniques and algorithms. AI relies upon "**AI agents**" that interact with the environment to learn and adapt, where learning is guided by the definition of the rewards and penalties (positive and negative incentives) associated with each action. AI leverages DL, ML, and/or RL to guide the AI agent to learn from continuous engagement with its environment in order to create the intelligence necessary to maximize current and future rewards (see *Figure 6.7*).

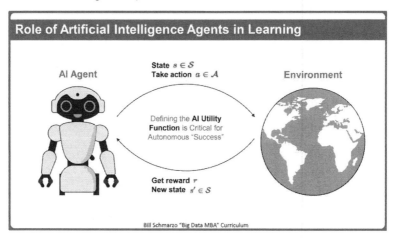

Figure 6.7: Role of AI Agents in Learning

The rewards or incentives against which the AI agent seeks to optimize are framed by the definition of "value" as defined in the **AI Utility Function**. The AI Utility Function provides the objective criterion that measures the progress and success of an AI rational agent's actions. In order to ensure the AI agent exhibits the appropriate "intelligence" to make the "right" decisions, the AI Utility Function must cover a holistic definition of "value" including consideration of financial, operational, customer satisfaction, societal, environmental, and spiritual factors (see *Figure 6.8*).

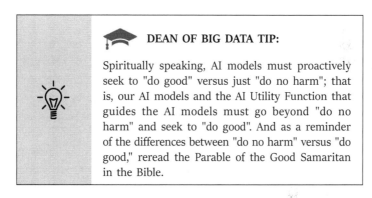

> **DEAN OF BIG DATA TIP:**
>
> Spiritually speaking, AI models must proactively seek to "do good" versus just "do no harm"; that is, our AI models and the AI Utility Function that guides the AI models must go beyond "do no harm" and seek to "do good". And as a reminder of the differences between "do no harm" versus "do good," reread the Parable of the Good Samaritan in the Bible.

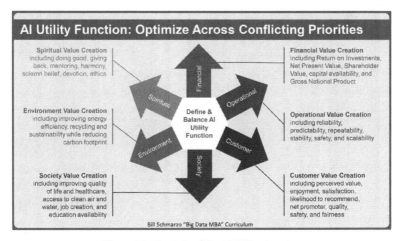

Figure 6.8: The Role of the AI Utility Function

To summarize, *AI is guided by AI agents that seek to make "intelligent" decisions based upon "value" as has been defined by the AI Utility Function.*

Case Study #1: Google TensorFlow

The Google Search business may be the most profitable business in the world. Google enjoys outrageous profit margins and market share domination of the world's #1 digital marketing media—search marketing. And the tool that drives Google's search marketing dominance is **TensorFlow**.

TensorFlow is an open-source ML and DL software library developed and managed by Google for data processing and model-driven programming across a range of tasks. Not only does Google's use of TensorFlow serve as the basis for its insanely profitable search engine, but TensorFlow also supports many other Google services including Photos (it auto-magically groups your photos into storyboards or collages), spoken word recognition (natural language processing), and foreign language translation (handy for me as I frequently travel internationally). Figure 6.9 depicts TensorFlow's high-level architecture, which is arguably the foundation for everything that makes Google money.

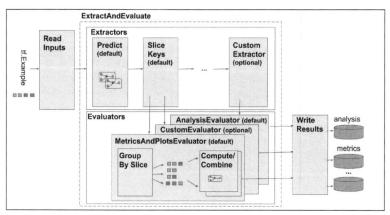

Figure 6.9: TensorFlow Architecture

So, why on God's green earth would Google open-source what may be their single most important technology? What does Google know that the other 99.99% of organizations don't know? I don't roam the hallowed hallways of Google or have access to any insider secrets as to its future business models, but it sure does make one ponder why they would give away the very engine that fuels their obscenely lucrative search business.

And, moreover, why would Google open-source TensorFlow and make it accessible to everyone—researchers, scientists, machine learning experts, students, and even its competitors? The December 1, 2015 Forbes article *"Reasons Why Google's Latest AI-TensorFlow is Open Sourced"* gives us a glimpse into the answer:

"In order to keep up with this influx of data and expedite the evolution of its machine learning engine, Google has open sourced its engine TensorFlow."

Google is using an open-source strategy to get more folks to continuously test, learn, refine, and adapt TensorFlow in new ways that ultimately will improve TensorFlow's predictive effectiveness and reliability and make the products upon which TensorFlow is based even more effective. Google open-sourced TensorFlow to gain the accumulated learning gleaned from thousands of new use cases to improve the predictive and operational effectiveness of the platform that runs Google's business, and therefore makes Google more profitable. Yeah, in the end, it's always about the 4 M's of Big Data: "Make Me More Money."

By open-sourcing TensorFlow, Google can get the large community of Data Scientists to ultimately make the engine that runs Google's different businesses even more powerful than Google could on its own. Google is letting the world—including their competitors—improve the very engine that powers Google's business models and in effect, challenging anyone to beat them at their own game... a ballsy yet brilliant move.

Case Study #2: Tesla Autonomous Vehicles

"If you buy a Tesla today, I believe you're buying an appreciating asset, not a depreciating asset."

– Elon Musk

Think about that statement for a second... you're buying an appreciating asset, not a depreciating asset. Wait, according to **Generally Accepted Accounting Principles (GAAP)**, assets depreciate not appreciate. So, what is causing this asset to appreciate, not depreciate, in value? It's likely courtesy of Tesla's FSD AI-based Autopilot brain (a composable, reusable, continuously learning analytic module). Tesla cars become "smarter" and consequently more valuable with every mile that each of the 600,000+ FSD Autopilot-equipped Tesla cars are driven.

Elon Musk's statement that Tesla autonomous cars appreciate in value (that is, they become more valuable) is a result of the collective knowledge/wisdom/intelligence gleaned from the operational and driving data that is being captured across the growing fleet of Tesla autonomous cars every day. What is experienced and learned by one Tesla car is validated, codified, and shared with every other Tesla car, making the collective of Tesla cars more reliable, efficient, safe, and intelligent, and therefore more valuable.

Imagine a mindset of leveraging AI with real-time, detailed operational and operator data to create products (vehicles, trains, cranes, compressors, chillers, turbines, drills, and CAT and MRI scanners) whose value appreciates with usage because the products are getting more reliable, more predictive, efficient, effective, safe, and consequently more valuable. That is H-U-G-E!

An asset that appreciates in value through usage and learning is yet another example of how leading organizations can exploit the unique characteristics of digital assets that not only never deplete or wear out and can be used across an unlimited number of use cases at a near-zero marginal cost, but also appreciate in value the more that asset is used (see *Figure 6.10*).

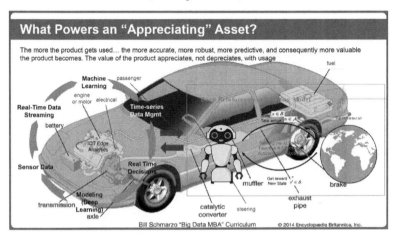

Figure 6.10: AI Powers "Learning" Products or Assets

Tesla is aggregating all of the cars' operational and driving data in the Tesla cloud, where it is running even more driving simulations to continuously train the autonomous FSD Autopilot analytic module. Tesla collects data about how FSD would handle different driving scenarios even when the feature isn't turned on (thereby creating labeled data for new use cases). Yes, Tesla cars log instances where the FSD Autopilot would have taken an action even when it's not turned on so that the car can continuously learn from the human operators. This "shadow mode" of data collection enables the collection of driving data even when the driver hasn't turned on the Autopilot mode.

This new intelligence then gets propagated back to each individual car resulting in new and improved capabilities—passing slow-moving cars, navigating to the off ramp, maneuvering around traffic accidents and debris on the roads, traversing water puddles after rain, and so on. As a result, Tesla cars are continuously learning and adapting and are becoming more valuable through economic compounding (see *Figure 6.11*).

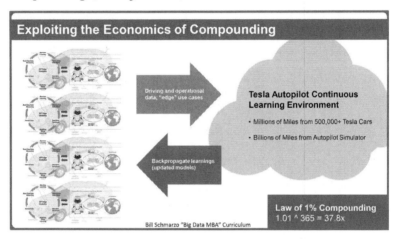

Figure 6.11: Exploiting the Economics of Compounding

It is the usage of the cars that drives the cars' aggregated appreciation in value; the power of compounding small improvements in reliability, efficiency, and safety that quickly build into an impressive overall improvement. And for folks who don't appreciate the power of compounding, a 1% improvement compounded 365 times equals a 37.8x overall improvement ($1.01^{365} = 37.78$). Now those are numbers that one can really *appreciate!*

Tesla autonomous cars are exploiting the capabilities of Artificial Intelligence to create continuously learning and adapting autonomous vehicles that get more reliable, more efficient, safer, more intelligent, and consequently more valuable through usage...with minimal human intervention!

Simply brilliant.

The Autonomous Holy Grail of AI

The Holy Grail of AI (and one of the keys to reaching Phase 5: Digital Transformation of the Big Data Business Model Maturity Index) is the creation of autonomous products, processes, policies, and systems that continuously learn and adapt with no, or little, human intervention. It's automation, but with a brain that is continuously learning and adapting based upon the ever-changing environment in which these assets operate.

DEAN OF BIG DATA TIP:

The other key for organizations to reach Phase 5: Digital Transformation is empowering the front lines of the organization. We will cover the challenge of cultural empowerment in *Chapter 9, Creating a Culture of Innovation Through Empowerment.*

If your organization seeks to reach this phase of creating autonomous products, process, policies, and systems that continuously learn and adapt with minimal human intervention—of creating autonomous assets that appreciate in value the more that they are used—then here are a few laws that we can take away from the Google TensorFlow and Tesla FSD case studies that can be applied to your organization's digital transformation journey:

- **Autonomous Law #1**: Autonomous entities needs lots and lots of real-time, granular (big) data from a robust and diverse set of use cases against which to apply AI and Deep RL in order to continuously learn.

- **Autonomous Law #2**: Autonomous entities leverage fail-safe environments (that is, games and simulations) to train the AI agents to operate, learn, and adapt across a wide variety of use cases within a constantly changing environment.

- **Autonomous Law #3**: Autonomous entities are complex systems comprised of numerous, sometimes conflicting operational subsystems, all of which are seeking to optimize their own performance, across which the autonomous entity must seek to optimize.

- **Autonomous Law #4**: For an entity to truly be autonomous, that entity must integrate, interoperate, and optimize across all of these subsystems to maximize its AI utility function (maximizing rewards while minimizing penalties) with minimal human intervention.

- **Autonomous Law #5**: Autonomous projects won't "fail" because of the AI technologies, they'll "fail" because of poorly constructed AI Utility Functions where "failure" includes the second- and third-degree unintended consequences from the autonomous agent's actions. Hey, the Terminator was only doing what its AI Utility Function told it to optimize against!

Summary

Organizations must avoid the cheap allure of "orphaned analytics"—building one-off analytics that address immediate business needs but lack the data science engineering effort to build composable, reusable, continuously learning analytic modules. The ability to leverage AI to create assets that appreciate (not depreciate) in value the more that they are used is a business and economics game-changer. Let's just open our eyes and take a lesson from Google and Tesla about becoming more effective at leveraging data and analytics to power (or even reinvent) their business models.

If you want to change the game, you need to change your frame.

Further Reading

1. *Bill Schmarzo, How to Avoid Orphaned Analytics*, 1 August 2016: `https://www.linkedin.com/pulse/how avoid-orphaned-analytics-bill-schmarzo/`

2. *Bill Schmarzo, "Leaving Money on the Table and the Economics of Composable, Reusable Analytic Modules"*, 13 February 2020: `https://www.linkedin.com/pulse/leaving-money-table-economics-composable-reusable-modules-schmarzo/`

3. *Bill Schmarzo, Creating Assets that Appreciate, Not Depreciate, in Value Thru Continuous Learning – Part II*, 8 December 2019: `https://www.linkedin.com/pulse/creating-assets-appreciate-depreciate-value-thru-part-bill-schmarzo/`

4. *Cleans a Whole Level of Your Home | Roomba® 900 series | iRobot®*: `https://www.youtube.com/watch?v=oj3Vawn-kRE`

5. *Tensorflow Model Analysis Architecture*: `https://www.tensorflow.org/tfx/model_analysis/architecture`

6. *Jordon Golson, Tesla's new Autopilot will run in 'shadow mode' to prove that it's safer than human driving*, 19 October 2016: `https://www.theverge.com/2016/10/19/13341194/tesla-autopilot-shadow-mode-autonomous-regulations`

7. *Bill Schmarzo, Creating Autonomous Entities: Optimizing Systems of Subsystems*, 4 November 2019: `https://www.datasciencecentral.com/profiles/blogs/creating-autonomous-entities-optimizing-systems-of-subsystems`

Homework

1. How fluent in Deep Learning and Artificial Intelligence is **your organization?**

AI pilots but no organizational strategy	Have AI business strategy with budget	Deploying AI-enabled product	Deploying AI-based autonomous assets						
1	2	3	4	5	6	7	8	9	10

Score:_____ Assessment: _____

_____

_____

_____

2. How fluent in Deep Learning and Artificial Intelligence are **you?**

Starting AI/DL research and reading	Taking online courses on AI / DL	Have developed a neural network model	Have deployed a neural network model						
1	2	3	4	5	6	7	8	9	10

Score:_____ Assessment: _____

_____

_____

_____

3. Have you thought about where within your organization Artificial Intelligence could apply to create assets that appreciate in value?

Started brainstorming with managers	Have created business case with return on investment	Have created asset prototype using AI	Have deployed AI-enabled product / service

1	2	3	4	5	6	7	8	9	10

Score:_____ Assessment: _____

_____

_____

_____

7

THE SCHMARZO ECONOMIC DIGITAL ASSET VALUATION THEOREM

The "Economies of Learning" are more powerful than the "Economies of Scale."

In *Chapter 6, The Economies of Artificial Intelligence*, we learned that we can use **Artificial Intelligence** (**AI**) to create assets that appreciate, not depreciate, in value the more those assets are used. Both Google TensorFlow and Tesla's AI-powered **Full Self-Driving** (**FSD**) autonomous Autopilot module are continuously learning and adapting analytic assets that, through usage, are continuously getting more reliable, accurate, efficient, predictive, safe... and valuable.

In this chapter, I'll introduce the **Schmarzo Economic Digital Asset Valuation Theorem** (my attempt for a Nobel Prize in Economics). But before I deep dive into explaining the details behind the theorem, let's first have a little economics lesson.

The Economies of Scale

Historically, organizations sought competitive advantage through business models that exploited the Economics of Scale. Economies of Scale manifest themselves in cost advantages that enterprises can enjoy due to their scale of operation (typically driven by the volume of output), with cost per unit of output decreasing with increasing production. Organizations leveraged the world of "mass"—mass procurement, mass production, mass distribution, mass marketing, mass media—to erect insurmountable barriers of entry to competitors (see *Figure 7.1*):

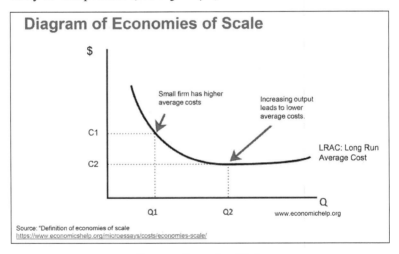

Figure 7.1: Economies of Scale

Volume affords an enormous competitive advantage. As the Quantity (**Q**) or volume of items manufactured increases from **Q1** to **Q2**, the Cost (**$**) of the item decreases from **C1** to **C2**.

Over the long run, the **Long Run Average Cost** (**LRAC**) continues to decrease, though LRAC can creep back up due to inefficient overuse of resources (like overtime). Economies of Scale not only spread large fixed costs over high volumes of output to drive down costs per unit but also create a formidable barrier to entry that hinders new competitors from easily entering markets. See *Figure 7.2* for an example of how Coca-Cola has leveraged Economies of Scale to defend the brand's dominant market share position:

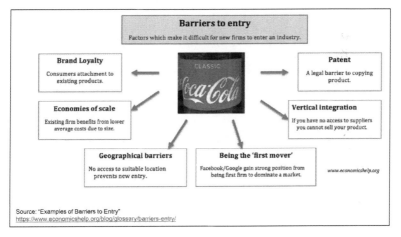

Figure 7.2: Coca Cola Barriers to Entry

There is, however, a disadvantage to Economies of Scale—the large fixed investments impede an organization's agility and nimbleness, and ultimately preclude the organization from exploiting the **Economies of Learning**.

The Economies of Learning

The book *The Lean Startup* by *Eric Ries* highlights the power of the **Economies of Learning** concept with a story about stuffing 100 envelopes.

Instead of the traditional Economies of Scale approach associated with the division and specialization of labor—first folding all 100 newsletters, then stuffing all 100 of the newsletters into envelopes, then sealing all 100 envelopes and finally putting stamps on all 100 of the envelopes—Ries discovered the optimal way to manage these tasks is to fold, stuff, seal, and stamp one newsletter at a time. The reason why this "one at a time" approach is more effective is because:

1. From a process perspective, you can learn what's most efficient by conducting the collective tasks one after the other and immediately reapply those learnings in the next instance (like inserting a newsletter crease first into the envelope so the newsletter doesn't catch on the envelope flap).

2. You don't have to wait until the end to realize that you have made a costly or fatal error in the process that negates all the effort (like folding all of the envelopes the wrong way before you realize that they won't fit into the envelopes).

 DEAN OF BIG DATA TIP:

The use-case-by-use-case deployment approach not only exploits the rapid learning, sharing, and reapplication of those learnings to future use cases but also enables organizations to deliver a compelling **Return on Investment** (**ROI**) on each use case as they build out their data and analytics assets. This approach puts an end to risky "Big Bang" analytics projects (because as *Eric* Reis states in *The Lean Startup*, *"fatal project errors are not uncovered until the end of the project"*).

Organizations can exploit the **Economies of Learning** in how they manage their data science capabilities and the associated development of their data and analytic assets by deploying data science projects on a use-case-by-use-case basis.

This way, they can share and reapply data and analytic learnings from one use case more easily to the next use case. This "**Thinking Like a Data Scientist**" methodology (see my book *The Art of Thinking Like a Data Scientist* for more details on the methodology, including worksheets, templates, and hands-on exercises) revolves around this use case-by-use case approach, which facilitates rapid learning, sharing, and reapplication of that learning to future use cases.

The "**Thinking Like a Data Scientist**" methodology, which enables this use case-by-use case deployment and learning approach, requires organizational buy-in, focus, patience, and alignment to identify, validate, value, and prioritize the use cases against which to apply this use case-by-use case deployment process (see *Figure 7.3*):

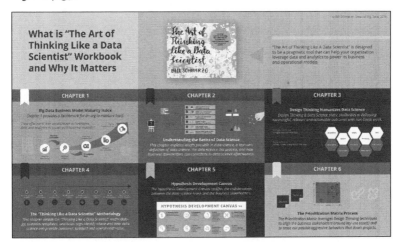

Figure 7.3: "The Art of Thinking Like a Data Scientist"

So now that we understand that the sharing and reapplication of learnings is a powerful concept—that the **Economies of Learning** are more powerful than the **Economies of Scale**—let's review the 3 economic effects that power the Schmarzo Economic Digital Asset Valuation Theorem.

Digital Economics Effect #1: Marginal Costs Flatten

Since data never depletes, never wears out and can be reused against an unlimited number of use cases at near-zero marginal cost, reusing "curated" data and analytic modules reduce the marginal costs for future use cases (see *Figure 7.4*).

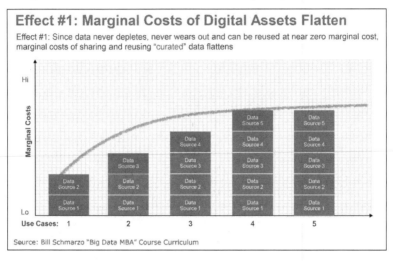

Figure 7.4: Effect #1: Marginal Costs of Digital Assets Flatten

For organizations to realize the economic benefits of *Effect #1*, they must actively work to stomp out data silos that inhibit the sharing of organizational data. This is the biggest inhibitor of the economic value of data, as discussed in *Chapter 4, University of San Francisco Economic Value of Data Research Paper*. Sharing and reusing the "curated" data enables the organization to exploit the data lake to flatten marginal costs. "Curated" data is a dataset in which investments have been made to improve the data's cleanliness, completeness, accuracy, granularity, and latency; in which the data has been enhanced through data transformations, data enrichment, and metadata management; and in which the dataset is formally governed to ensure compliance in its usage.

If organizations are seeking to drive down their data lake costs via the sharing and reuse of data across multiple use cases, then putting curated data into the data lack is critical. Randomly loading raw data into your data lake just turns your data lake into a "data swamp" and forces each use case to incur the full cost of data preparation every time the data is reused. However, by loading the data lake with curated data that has been validated by its application in a use case, the data lake soon becomes the organization's Collaborative Value Creation Platform that facilitates the sharing of data across the organization, and across multiple use cases.

 DEAN OF BIG DATA TIP:

Data silos are the killers of the economic value of data. Data silos are data repositories that remain under the control of one department and are isolated from the rest of the organization, which inhibits organizations from maximizing the economic value of data realized from the sharing and reusing the same data across multiple use cases.

Digital Economics Effect #2: Economic Value of Digital Assets Grows

Sharing and reusing data and analytic modules accelerate use case time-to-value and de-risks use case implementation (see *Figure 7.5*).

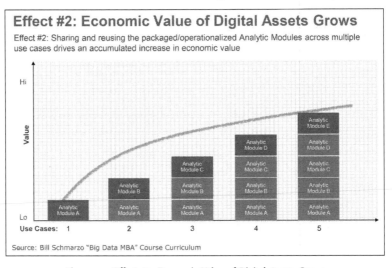

Figure 7.5: Effect #2: Economic Value of Digital Assets Grows

Reuse of the data courtesy of the organization's data lake is one factor that can accelerate use case time-to-value and de-risk use case implementations. For example, one might find that it takes 9 months to complete the first use case because the organization needs to pay the price of creating curated data (including associated data preparation, data management, data transformation, data enrichment, and data governance) that is housed in the organization's data lake. And then maybe the second use case takes 6 months because while the organization can reuse the data in the data lake from *Use Case #1*, it might need to add another curated data source to support *Use Case #2* (and so forth as the organization builds out its data lake, or collaborative value creation platform, one use case at a time).

DEAN OF BIG DATA TIP:

The creation of a coherent use case roadmap is critical and should be ROI-driven. I covered how organizations can go about the process of identifying, validating, valuing, and prioritizing their business and operational use cases in my book *The Art of Thinking Like a Data Scientist.*

Also, as we discussed in *Chapter 6, The Economics of Artificial Intelligence*, orphaned analytics negate the time-to-value and implementation de-risking advantages because orphaned analytics cannot be reused across multiple use cases. Remember, orphaned analytics are one-off analytics developed for a specific business need, but the organization never applied the engineering discipline to "operationalize" and scale the analytics for reuse across multiple use cases. Unfortunately, many organizations lack an overarching architecture and the analytic module packaging process (also discussed in *Chapter 6, The Economics of Artificial Intelligence*) to ensure that the resulting analytics can be reused across multiple use cases.

To realize the benefits of the Digital Economics *Effect #2*, organizations need to focus their analytics development efforts on creating, packaging, and operationalizing their composable, reusable, continuously learning analytic modules, to avoid the fate of orphaned analytics and to facilitate the sharing and reuse of the analytic modules across multiple use cases. This accelerates use case time-to-value and de-risks use case implementation.

Digital Economics Effect #3: Economic Value of Digital Assets Accelerates

Across multiple use cases, the value of an analytic module's predictive "refinement" accelerates economic value because the continuous predictive and operational improvements of a specific analytic module lifts the value of all use cases that have used that same analytic module (see *Figure 7.6*):

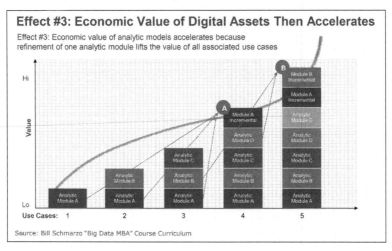

Figure 7.6: Effect #3: Economic Value of Digital Assets Then Accelerates

Let me explain *Digital Economics Effect #3*—the analytic module predictive "refinement" effect—in *Figure 7.6*:

- Let's say that we have created Analytic Module A, which was used to support *Use Cases #1, #2,* and *#3*. Now let's say that in *Use Case #4*, the data science team "refines" or improves the predictive accuracy and effectiveness of Analytic Module A through new data enrichment techniques, or improved hyperparameter optimization, or a more effective new neural network technique.

As a result of this data science "refinement" work, Analytic Module A now delivers a more accurate, more efficient, and more reliable prediction. The predictive "refinement" or improvement of Analytic Module A for *Use Case #4* consequently ripples back through *Use Cases #1, #2,* and *#3,* improving the predictive accuracy and reliability of each of those use cases at near-zero marginal cost. As an example, let's say that Analytic Module A is for Anomaly Detection, which we will designate Anomaly Detection 1.0. When the predictive accuracy, effectiveness and reliability of the Anomaly Detection Analytic Module is refined or improved for *Use Case #4*, the Anomaly Detection Analytic Module evolves into Anomaly Detection 2.0. Now all the prior use cases that used Anomaly Detection 1.0 (*Use Cases #1, #2.,* and *#3*) now inherit the predictive accuracy, effectiveness and reliability improvements of Anomaly Detection 2.0 at a near-zero marginal cost (with proper regression testing). This point of economic value acceleration is reflected by point (A) in *Figure 7.6.*

- The same Analytic Module "refinement" effect occurs when the predictive accuracy and effectiveness of Analytic Module B (which we will designate Remaining Useful Life 1.0) is "refined" or improved for the benefit of *Use Case #5* (Remaining Useful Life 2.0), and the economic benefits of the Analytic Module B "refinement" (reflected as point (B) in *Figure 7.6*) ripple through the previous use cases that used Analytic Module B (*Use Cases #2, #3,* and *#4*).

DEAN OF BIG DATA TIP:

Analytic Module predictive "refinement" could be driven by new data sources, more granular data, reduced data latency, data enrichment, data transformation, data blending, improvements in data quality and data completeness, new analytic algorithms, improved hyperparameter optimization, or any of a litany of data engineering and data science analytic module improvements.

This overall Analytic Model "refinement" economic effect is shown by the increasing angle of the slope in *Figure 7.6*. But this economic value acceleration cannot occur if the applications are not built as composable, reusable, continuously learning Analytic Modules that can be shared, reused, adapted, and "refined" (for continuous learning).

This is the heart of Tesla's AI-enabled autonomous vehicle business model. Tesla's AI strategy seeks continuous improvements in the predictive effectiveness and reliability in the AI-driven FSD Autopilot analytic module that creates assets that appreciate, not depreciate, the more that the asset is used. And small 1% improvements in the predictive effectiveness and reliability yielded by one use case can be aggregated by the AI simulator in the cloud and backpropagated to each of the other 600,000 Tesla vehicles. Brilliant.

Now we can complete the *Figure 5.5* that we introduced in *Chapter 5, The Economic Value of Data Theorems* (see *Figure 7.7*).

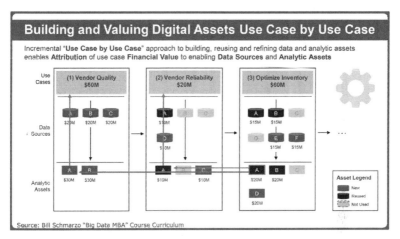

Figure 7.7: Updated Valuing Data Assets Example

In *Figure 7.7*, the financial value of the use case has been allocated to the supporting analytic modules. For example, *Use Case #1* ("Improve Vendor Product Quality") is worth $60M annually and requires 2 analytic modules (A and B) to optimize that use case. Using a straight-line financial allocation approach, we can allocate $30M of value ($60 / 2 = $30M) to each of the 2 enabling analytic modules for *Use Case #1*. We use the same straight-line allocation of the financial value of *Use Cases #2* and *#3* to the enabling analytic modules A, B, C, and D in *Figure 7.7*.

The most powerful and game-changing factor in *Figure 7.7* is if there is an improvement in the predictive accuracy or operational effectiveness of analytic module A in support of *Use Case #3* (from using new analytic techniques, or feature engineering, or hyperparameter optimization or such like), the prior use cases that also used analytic module A (*Use Cases #1* and *#2*) reap the financial benefits in the predictive accuracy and operational effectiveness of analytic module A.

Implementing the Schmarzo Economic Digital Asset Valuation Theorem

The investments that organizations must make to exploit the Schmarzo Economic Digital Asset Valuation Theorem include:

- Creating a single centralized curated data lake, or collaborative value creation platform, that facilitates the sharing and reuse of the organization's data assets. Curated data is data in which there has been investment to improve the data's cleanliness, completeness, accuracy, granularity and latency, enhanced metadata, and data usage governance to ensure compliance in its use and continued enrichment. The data in the data lake should be cataloged and indexed to support easy accessibility, reuse and refinement with minimal incremental investment.

- Investing in the data science engineering work to create composable, reusable, **continuously learning analytic modules** where the sharing, reuse, learning, and resulting "refinement" of the analytic modules can be used to accelerate the organization's customer, product, and operational value creation across multiple use cases. These analytic modules leverage AI to create analytic assets that appreciate, not depreciate, in value the more that these analytic modules are used.

Organizations must also stomp out the killers of the economic value of your organization's data and analytic assets, including:

- **Data silos**—data repositories that remain under the control of one department, isolated from the rest of the organization. They are consequently never shared or reused across multiple use cases and thusly cannot benefit from the data economic multiplier effect.

- **Orphaned analytics**—one-off analytics developed to address a specific business need, but never "operationalized" or packaged for reuse in future use cases and cannot benefit from an environment of continuous learning and adapting across multiple use cases.

- **Management ignorance** that still views data as a necessary cost of doing business (and consequently, a cost to be minimized) versus the economic game-changer to reinvent current business models, re-engineer industry value chains, and disintermediate customer relationships (that's our set up for *Chapter 8, The 8 Laws of Digital Transformation*).

Summary

The **Schmarzo Economic Digital Asset Valuation Theorem** provides a compelling economic reason for organizations to make the necessary investments in the creation, sharing, reuse, and continuous refinement of their data and analytic assets—assets that not only never deplete, never wear out and can be used across an unlimited number of use cases at near-zero marginal cost, but assets that appreciate in value the more that they are used.

In summary, by reusing the datasets and analytics modules, organizations thereby not only maintain but increase the economic value of their data and analytic modules. This affords organizations a once-in-a-generation opportunity to exploit the unique economic characteristics of their data, and analytic modules to derive and drive new sources of customer, product, and operational value buried in their data.

Following the guidelines outlined in this book and highlighted in this chapter, organizations can reap the game-changing effects articulated by the **Schmarzo Economic Digital Asset Valuation Theorem**:

- **Effect #1:** Since data never depletes, never wears out, and can be reused at near-zero marginal cost, reusing "curated" data and analytic modules reduce marginal costs for each new use case.

- **Effect #2:** Sharing and reusing the data and analytic modules accelerate use case time-to-value and de-risks implementation.

- **Effect #3:** Across multiple use cases, the value of analytic model "refinement" accelerates economic impact, because predictive "refinement" of one analytic module lifts the value of all associated use cases.

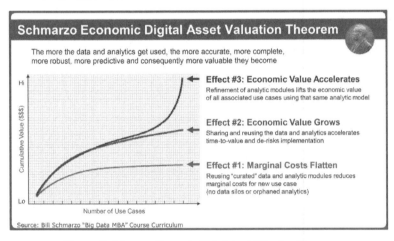

Figure 7.8: Schmarzo Economic Digital Asset Valuation Theorem

I am already feeling the weight of "*The Medal for the Sveriges Riksbank Prize in Economic Sciences in Memory of Alfred Nobel*" dangling around my neck. Par-tay in Sweden!

Further Reading

1. *Tejvan Pettinger, Definition of economies of scale, Economics Help*, 28 June 2019: `https://www.economicshelp.org/microessays/costs/economies-scale/`

2. *Examples of Barriers to Entry, Economics Help*: `https://www.economicshelp.org/blog/glossary/barriers-entry/`

3. *The Art of Thinking Like a Data Scientist*: `https://deanofbigdata.com/shop?olsPage=products%2Fthe-art-of-thinking-like-a-data-scientist`

Homework

1. Do you have a culture of sharing your data and analytic assets across organizational borders?

Culture of siloed decision making	Small number of collaborative teams	Sharing culture bolstered by Design Thinking	Management incentives for sharing

1	2	3	4	5	6	7	8	9	10

Score:_____ Assessment: _____

_____

_____

_____

2. Do you have the organizational fortitude to embrace the economic potential of data assets?

No interest in leveraging data assets	Cross-function pilot to share data assets	Methodology for determining data value	Management incentives to share data assets

1	2	3	4	5	6	7	8	9	10

Score:_____ Assessment: _____

_____

_____

_____

3. Is your data lake a Collaborative Value Creation Platform?

Multiple data lakes/data warehouses	Single data lake but no governance process	Data lake fully cataloged, managed, and governed	Data valuation method integrated with data lake

1	2	3	4	5	6	7	8	9	10

Score:_____ Assessment: _____

_____

_____

_____

4. Do you build composable, repeatable, and continuously learning analytic modules?

Few advanced analytics efforts	Growing advanced analytic projects but no reuse	Engineering methodology for analytic modules	Management incentives to reuse analytic modules

1	2	3	4	5	6	7	8	9	10

Score:_____ Assessment: _____

_____

_____

_____

BILL SCHMARZO
Dean of Big Data

8

THE 8 LAWS OF DIGITAL TRANSFORMATION

Finally, the Holy Grail. Nirvana. Serendipity's Golden Opulence Sundae (nice). Shangri-La. The Cubs winning the World Series. The "ultimate operative state" every modern organization seeks to achieve...**Digital Transformation**. But what exactly *is* Digital Transformation?

Digital Transformation is the creation of a continuously learning and adapting, AI-driven, and human-empowered business model that seeks to identify, codify, and operationalize actionable customer, product, and operational insights (propensities) in order to optimize (reinvent) operational efficiency, enhance customer value creation, mitigate operational and compliance risk, and create new revenue opportunities.

In this chapter, we'll pull together all the aspects of digital transformation we've discussed so far—with the concept of "human empowerment" to be covered in *Chapter 9, Creating a Culture of Innovation Through Empowerment*—into an actionable yet pragmatic plan to help organizations digitally transform their business and operational models. Digital Transformation is especially crucial as world events and developments, such as the COVID-19 pandemic, highlight the need for organizations to strive towards digital transformation expeditiously in order to survive.

Unfortunately, many organizations think that Digital Transformation simply means digitalizing their customer engagements and business operations; that is, replacing human analog processes with device or application digital processes. But that's not nearly sufficient to truly achieve digital transformation.

Organizations that are going to survive, and thrive, in the 21st century must go beyond just "digitalizing" their customer engagements and business operations. Organizations must transition to a business model that proactively seeks to uncover, codify, and leverage granular customer, product, and operational insights (propensities) around which they can **reinvent** key business processes, reduce operational and compliance risks, uncover new revenue opportunities, and create a more compelling, differentiated customer experience.

To help guide organizations along their digital transformation journey, I have come up with these "**Digital Transformation (DX) Laws**"; laws based on repeated observations that describe or predict a range of natural phenomena. These "Digital Transformation Laws" come courtesy of several customer engagements; engagements where organizations are pursuing digital transformation but get waylaid by unexpected obstacles along that journey (picture the "Jason and the Argonauts" movie...the original not the awful remake).

DX Law #1: It's About Business Models, Not Just Business Processes

Digital Transformation is about reinventing and innovating business models, not just optimizing existing business processes.

Solely optimizing existing business processes is a "**paving the cow path**" mindset, where organizations simply apply new digital technologies to replace existing human-intensive operational processes, without taking into full consideration where and how new sources of customer, product, and operational value can be created. And while "paving the cow path" can yield marginal improvements in your business model (a Horizon 1 effect that we will discuss later in the chapter), marginal improvements won't win the day from a business model reinvention and digital transformation perspective.

Digital Transformation is about creating and leveraging new **digital assets** (data, analytics, and insights or propensities about customers, products, and operations) to **reinvent** your **business model** and create new sources of competitive differentiation. Organizations who have committed to Digital Transformation are looking to leverage these digital assets to create "economic moats."

Warren Buffett, the investor extraordinaire, popularized the term "**economic moat**" to refer to a *business' ability to maintain competitive advantages over its competitors (through process and technology innovation and patents) to protect its long-term profits and market share from competing firms*; to reinvent industry value chains and disintermediate competitors' customer relationships. Organizations who are not able to create economic moats, well, it doesn't end well for them (see *Figure 8.1*).

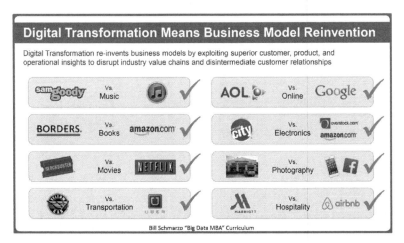

Figure 8.1: Digital Transformation Means Business Model Reinvention

Beware of the senior management team who believes that digital transformation will not affect their industry; that they are somehow magically protected by the artificially defined **Standard Industrial Classification** (**SIC**) industry borders. *Any industry that relies on customers should be concerned about digital transformation.* There are suppliers, channel partners, competitors from nearby industries, and even former customers who are ignoring those artificial industry borders and seeking to derive and drive new sources of value across the entirety of the customer journey, to identify opportunities to reinvent their customer value creation processes and disintermediate competitors' customer relationships. And yep, that means if your company doesn't undertake digital transformation, then your company could be the next victim (see *Figure 8.2*).

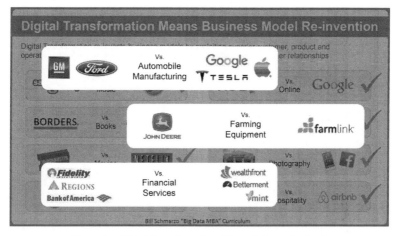

Figure 8.2: Digital Transformation...Whose Industry is Next?

DX Law #2: It's About Digital Transformation, Not Digitalization

Digital Transformation is about reinventing your customer engagements and business operations with continuously learning AI capabilities to derive and drive new sources of customer, product, service, and operational value.

Digital Transformation is more than just **digitalization**, which is the integration of digital technologies such as web-based apps, mobile devices, and sensors into existing operational processes. **digitalization** enhances or replaces human-centric processes with digital technologies, such as transmitting current patient health and wellness data to the cloud using mobile devices, apps, and sensors on a real-time, granular basis instead of requiring patients to physically travel to a care facility on an as-needed basis and have their vital health and wellness numbers manually recorded by a nurse (see *Figure 8.3*).

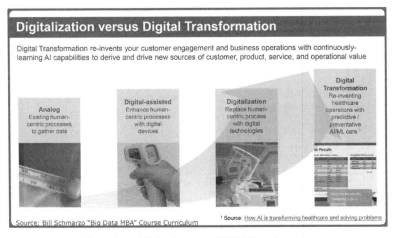

Figure 8.3: Digitalization versus Digital Transformation

Digital Transformation, on the other hand, leverages the growing wealth of Big Data and **Internet of Things** (**IoT**) with continuously learning AI to uncover new customer, product, service, and operational insights (propensities) to **reinvent** the organization's business models, to derive and drive new sources of customer, product, and operational value. Digital Transformation means creating a culture of continuous learning and operational adoption fueled at the front lines of customer and operational engagement, thereby creating an AI-powered organization whose value creation processes start at the organizational front lines.

DX Law #3: It's About Speaking the Language of Your Customers

Digital Transformation is about empathizing, ideating, validating, and quantifying the creators and inhibitors of customer value; it's about reinventing your business model to expand upon, exploit, and monetize those sources of customer value creation while eliminating the inhibitors of value creation.

Let's say that you are in the retail industry and looking to identify opportunities to combine digital technologies with customer usage insights (propensities) to eliminate barriers to customer value creation. That retailer would want to invest the time to empathize, ideate, validate, and quantify the sources and impediments of value creation for their customers. *Figure 8.4* provides an example of how a retailer could reinvent the customer value creation process by emphasizing the sources and eliminating the inhibitors of value creation.

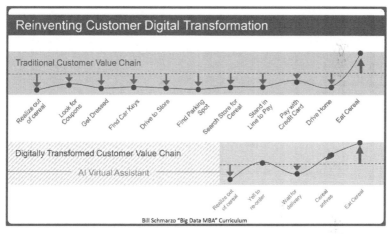

Figure 8.4: Traditional versus Digitally Transformed Customer Value Chain

The top part of *Figure 8.4* highlights today's analog-intensive customer engagement process. To demonstrate an example of this traditional customer journey, let's say I head to the pantry to grab a box of my favorite cereal, CAP'N CRUNCH'S© PEANUT BUTTER CRUNCH, only to discover to my utter dismay that the last box has been consumed by the kids. Trudging through the traditional customer journey to pick up another box, I'd encounter many inhibitors of value creation (represented by multiple red down arrows) as well as a single step that is a creator of customer value (represented by a single green up arrow). The result? When I'm out of the CAP'N and navigating the traditional customer journey, there ain't no joy in Mudville.

Now, take the bottom part of *Figure 8.4*: The **Digitally Transformed Customer Journey**, a simplified process where I say to my AI virtual assistant, "Hey knucklehead, please deliver two boxes of CAP'N CRUNCH here at the house pronto," and I'd pay for express service and receive the retailer's delivery within 30 minutes. Or better yet, what if the retailer developed an AI-based, continuously learning analytic model that interacts with my Analytic Profile comprised of my product usage propensities and preferences to proactively predict and prescriptively deliver 2 boxes of the CAP'N *before I realize that I'm out!*

The key point about *Figure 8.4?*

It isn't about just optimizing the existing ordering process; it isn't about just "paving the cow path." *Figure 8.4* demonstrates that digital transformation requires the complete rewiring (or reinvention)—of the organization's value creation process: from demand planning to procurement to quality control to logistics to inventory management to distribution to marketing to store operations to customer experience. And that complete rewiring or reinvention starts by developing an intimate understanding, appreciation, and empathy for your customers (and sometimes, even the customers of your customers).

What we're talking about here is learning to "speak the language of your customers." We will deep dive into this topic in *Chapter 9, Creating a Culture of Innovation Through Empowerment*, because the ability to "speak the language of your customers" may be the most important and fundamental step in realizing digital transformation success.

DX Law #4: It's About Creating New Digital Assets

Digital Transformation is about creating new digital assets—Analytic Profiles and analytic modules—that leverage customer, product and operational insights (propensities) to drive granular decisions and hyper-individualized prescriptive recommendations.

Organizations need to build new digital assets—Analytic Profiles (or Digital Twins) and composable, reusable, continuously learning analytic modules—that codify the customer, product, and operational insights (propensities) that provide the fuel for the organization's digital transformation.

As I discussed in *Chapter 3, A Review of Basic Economic Concepts,* **Analytic Profiles** capture detailed predictive insights (propensities) for each of the organization's key business or operational entities or assets that facilitate the delivery of hyper-individualized, predictive customer engagement and product usage and performance recommendations. For example, in the healthcare industry, Patient Analytic Profiles could digitally transform the healthcare industry by capturing granular patient, disease, treatment, medicine, fitness, wellness, doctor, and hospital analytic insights around which healthcare providers could digitally re-engineer and reinvent hyper-personalized healthcare services. These hyper-personalized healthcare services could include precision medicine, individualized welfare, remote diagnostics, predictive world population health, AI-driven digital wellness advisors, and prescriptive health and wellness recommendations (see *Figure 8.5*).

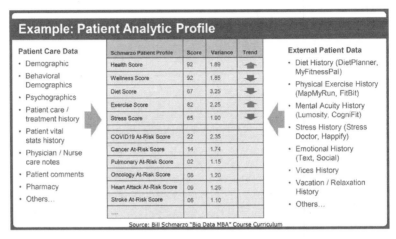

Figure 8.5: Sample Healthcare Patient Analytic Profile

The use of granular and predictive **Patient Analytic Profiles** could lead government healthcare agencies to replace blanket healthcare operational and policy decisions with hyper-personalized healthcare and wellness recommendations, which is the heart of the **Economic Value of Data Theorem #5** "Do more with less" that we discussed in *Chapter 5, The Economic Value of Data Theorems.*

And as I discussed in *Chapter 6, The Economics of Artificial Intelligence,* **Analytic Modules** are prebuilt, composable, reusable, continuously learning analytic assets that produce predefined business or operational outcomes built on a layer of technology abstraction that enables the orchestration and optimization of the underlying machine learning, reinforcement learning, and deep learning frameworks. Analytic Modules provide granular, predefined business and operational outcomes such as anomaly detection, customer propensity to buy, customer retention at-risk, predictive maintenance, operator skill evaluation, and scheduling optimization (see *Figure 8.6*).

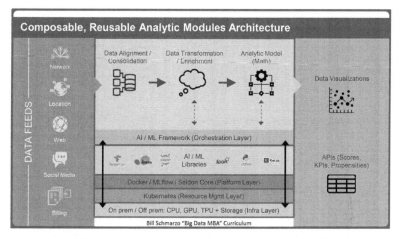

Figure 8.6: Composable, Reusable, Continuously learning Analytic Modules

Analytic Profiles and **Analytic Modules** are assets that economically behave like no other asset we have ever seen. These digital assets never wear out, never depreciate, and can be used across an unlimited number of use cases at near-zero marginal cost. And on top of that, these digital assets become more valuable the more they are used as their usage drives continuous learning and adaptation that leads to improvements in the predictive reliability, accuracy, and operational effectiveness of these digital assets.

DX Law #5: It's About Transitioning from Predicting to Prescribing to Autonomous

Digital Transformation is about predicting what's likely to happen, prescribing recommended actions, and continuously learning and adapting (autonomously) faster than your competition.

Digital Transformation is about creating an organization that continuously explores, learns, adapts, and relearns. Wash, rinse, repeat. Every customer engagement is an opportunity to learn more about the preferences and behaviors of that customer. Every product interaction or usage is an opportunity to learn more about the performance and behaviors of that product. Every employee, supplier, and partner engagement provides an opportunity to learn more about the effectiveness and efficiencies of your business operations.

As we discussed with the **Big Data Business Model Maturity Index** in *Chapter 1, The CEO Mandate: Become Value-driven, Not Data-driven*, to create a continuously learning intelligent organization, organizations need to master the transition from **reporting** to **predicting** to **prescribing** to **autonomous analytics**. That means proactively navigating up the three levels of the **Analytics Maturity Curve** (see *Figure 8.7*).

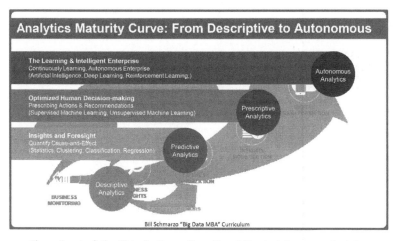

Figure 8.7: Analytics Maturity Curve: From Descriptive to Autonomous Analytics

This analytics maturity curve provides a guide to help organizations transition through the three levels of analytics maturity—from reporting to autonomous:

- **Level 1: Insights and Foresight.** This is the foundational level of advanced analytics that includes statistical analysis as well as the broad categories of predictive analytics (for example, clustering, classification, regression) and data mining. Level 1 leverages **descriptive** and **explorative** analytics to uncover the customer, product, and operational insights (propensities) buried in the data. The goal of Level 1 is to quantify cause-and-effect, determine confidence levels, and measure the goodness of fit with respect to the predictive insights.

- **Level 2: Optimized Human Decision Making.** The second level of advanced analytics includes supervised machine learning and unsupervised machine learning. Level 2 leverages **predictive** and **prescriptive** analytics that seek to predict what's likely to happen and then prescribe recommended or preventative actions. The goal of Level 2 is to create analytics that can learn and codify trends, patterns, and relationships; build predictive models that explain the trends, patterns, and relationships harvested from the data, and deliver prescriptive recommendations and actions without having to pre-program the business with static, operational (if-then type) rules.

- **Level 3: The Learning and Intelligent Enterprise.** The third level of advanced analytics includes artificial intelligence, reinforcement learning, and deep learning/neural networks. Level 3 leverages **automation** and **autonomous** analytics; analytics that continuously learn and adapt with minimal human intervention. These analytics seek to model the world around them—based upon the objectives as defined in the AI Utility Function—by continuously taking action, learning from that action, and adjusting the next action based upon the feedback from the previous action. Think of this as a giant game of "Hotter and Colder" where the analytics are continuously learning from each action and adjusting based upon the effectiveness of that action with respect to the operational goals (maximize rewards while minimizing costs) all with minimal human intervention.

Understanding and navigating the 3 levels of the **Analytics Maturity Curve** is likely a book in of itself. But remember that without the guiding principles of the **Big Data Business Model Maturity Index** and mastering the economic (wealth creation) aspects of the **Schmarzo Economic Digital Asset Valuation Theorem** against which to measure business and operational effectiveness, these advanced analytic technologies are nothing more than just shiny *enabling* technologies. These technologies are only the enablers of value creation; by themselves, they do not provide any value.

DX Law #6: It's About AI-driven Autonomous Operations and Policies

AI can enable more granular, relevant operational and policy decisions by continuously learning and adapting based upon most current environment situations...with minimal human intervention.

Policies are the foundation for any successful organization. They document the organizational principles, best practices, and compliance guidelines that aid decision-making in supporting the consistent and repeatable operations of the business. But most organization's policies are static, documented like a series of static **if-then rules** that are difficult to manage and even more difficult to update based upon changing business, economic, societal, cultural, and environmental conditions.

What if organizations could replace those static if-then types of policies with AI-based, continuously learning and adapting algorithms that learned and evolved based upon the constantly evolving state of the environment in which the business operates? The result would be an organization as nimble as the market and the world conditions dictate and would super-charge the organization's digital transformation (see *Figure 8.8*).

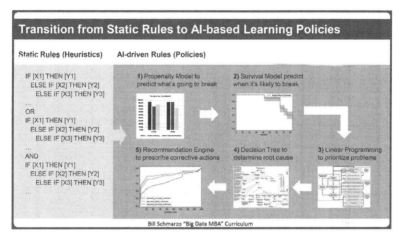

Figure 8.8: Transition from Static Rules to AI-based Learning Policies

"AI-driven Policies" are operational policies maintained by AI agents that take actions (or make decisions) that continuously seek to optimize, automate, adapt, and operationalize (scale) an organization's business and operational standard operating procedures within a constantly evolving environment with minimal human intervention.

Using **deep reinforcement learning**, we can transition from static rules to continuously learning and adapting autonomous policies that learn how to map any given situation (or state) to an action to reach a desired goal or objective with minimal human intervention. These autonomous policies would dynamically learn and adapt in response to constantly changing external factors such as pandemics, climate change, economic conditions, trade wars, and international conflicts, and give digitally transforming organizations a significant competitive advantage over organizations that operate their businesses using static policies.

DX Law #7: It's About Identifying, Codifying, and Operationalizing Sources of Value

The heart of Digital Transformation is the ability to identify, codify, and operationalize (scale) the sources of customer, product, and operational value within an environment that is continuously learning and adapting to ever-changing customer and market needs.

Digital Transformation knows no artificially defined industry borders. It seeks to uncover intimate and actionable "customer" insights no matter where that customer might be on their personal journey and use those customer insights to reinvent the organization's value creation processes (see *Figure 8.9*).

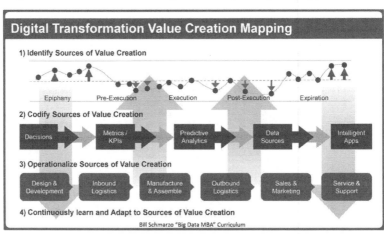

Figure 8.9: Digital Transformation Value Creation Mapping

Digital Transformation requires organizations to master four fundamental aspects of value creation:

- **Fundamental #1: Identify Sources of Value Creation**. Identify the sources of value creation with a customer-centric perspective (think "outside-in" view) that applies basic economic concepts to identify, validate, value, and prioritize the sources of customer (and market) value creation.

- **Fundamental #2: Codify Sources of Value Creation**. Use advanced analytics (AI, deep learning, machine learning, reinforcement learning) to codify customer, product, and operational insights (propensities) into digital assets – Analytic Profiles and composable, repeatable, continuously learning Analytic Modules.

- **Fundamental #3: Operationalize Sources of Value Creation**. Operationalize (scale) the sources of value creation through a production-centric perspective (think Michael Porter value chain analysis) that focuses on embedding the customer, product, and operational insights (propensities) into the organization's operational systems.

- **Fundamental #4: Continuously Learn and Adapt to Sources of Value Creation.** Create a continuously learning operational (with AI) and cultural (with empowered front-line employees) environment where the organization learns and adapts with every front-line customer engagement or operational interaction.

To execute against *Figure 8.9*, organizations will need to master a combination of design thinking (to identify the sources of value creation), economics (to value the sources of value creation), data science (to codify the sources of value creation), value chain analysis (to operationalize the sources of value creation), AI (to continuously learn and adapt to the sources of value creation), and cultural empowerment (which we will cover in *Chapter 9, Creating a Culture of Innovation Through Empowerment*).

DX Law #8: It's About the 3 Horizons of Digital Transformation

Create an Aspirational Vision to focus and prioritize the organization's immediate and long-term investments in customer, product, and operational value creation.

Unfortunately, most organizations do two things very poorly—prioritize and focus. Too many organizations "peanut butter" their precious transformational resources across too many "strategic" initiatives. Organizations don't fail due to a lack of "strategic" initiatives; organizations fail because they have too many. Which brings us to the final Digital Transformation Law and its importance in setting that **Aspirational Vision** towards which to direct and focus the organization's precious digital transformation resources and investments.

In 2000, McKinsey & Co proposed the "Three Horizons Portfolio Management Framework" as an approach that allows companies to manage a portfolio of projects for current and future growth. Then in 2015, Geoffrey Moore wrote his management strategy book "*Zone to Win*" that proposed a management framework to prioritize projects with the goal of sustaining the current business while investing in future businesses.

I've blended these two marvelous pieces of work (and I won't pretend to represent the depth of their work, so check out the footnotes for more details) into the **3 Horizons of Digital Transformation**. These 3 horizons in *Figure 8.10* provide a critical guide in helping organizations master the delicate balance between investing in today's business (which keeps the lights on) while simultaneously investing in tomorrow's digitally transformed business (which makes it worthwhile to keep the lights on today).

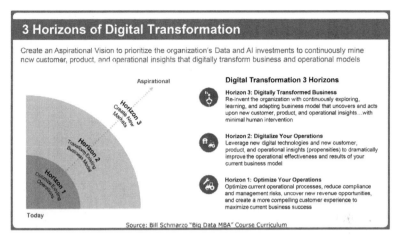

Figure 8.10: 3 Horizons of Digital Transformation

The **3 Horizons Framework** is designed to ensure that organizations don't get caught flat-footed by competitors (or aggressive, aspirational partners, suppliers, and even former customers) who are "thinking differently" about how digital transformation can reinvent their organization's business model based upon deriving and driving new sources of customer, product, and operational value.

Let's do a quick review of each of the horizons:

- **Horizon #1: Optimize Your Current Operations.** *Horizon #1* seeks to optimize current operational processes, reduce compliance and management risks, and create a more compelling customer experience in order to maximize current business success. It employs **descriptive** and **explorative** analytics to uncover the customer, product, and operational insights (propensities) buried in the data. Horizon 1 is focused on making money today, so the successful execution of your *Horizon #1* initiatives is critical for not only keeping the lights on but also provides the resources (money, people, and learning) that fund the organization's transition into *Horizon #2*.

- **Horizon #2: Digitalize Your Current Operations**. *Horizon #2* seeks to integrate new digital technologies with new customer, product, and operational insights (propensities) to dramatically improve the operational effectiveness of your current business model. Horizon 2 applies **predictive** and **Prescriptive** analytics that seek to predict what's likely to happen and prescribe recommended or preventative actions. Horizon 2 strives to master the creation of new digital assets (Analytic Profiles and Modules) that accelerate the ability to explore, learn, and exploit changing customer, market, and operational needs.

- **Horizon #3: Digitally Transform (Reinvent) Your Business Model**. *Horizon #3* seeks to reinvent the organization with a continuously learning and adapting business model that uncovers and acts upon the new customer, product, and operational insights (propensities) with minimal human intervention. Horizon 3 exploits the game-changing potential of **automation** and **autonomous** analytics that continuously learn, adapt, and reinvent the organization's business model as well as the industry's value chain. Horizon 3 seeks to create "economic moats" through superior customer, product, and operational insights (propensities) to disrupt current business models, re-engineer industry value chains, and disintermediate competitors' customer relationships.

Let's make this "**3 Horizons of Digital Transformation**" concept come to life with a simple example of how an Agriculture Equipment Manufacturer (since I am from Iowa) might leverage the 3 horizons to guide their Digital Transformation journey (see *Figure 8.11*).

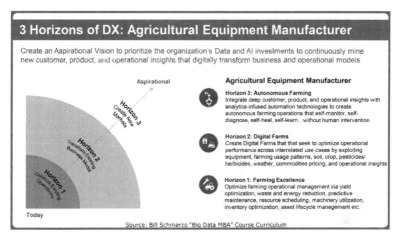

Figure 8.11: "3 Horizons of Digital Transformation" – Agricultural Equipment Manufacturer

Let's triage what the Agricultural Equipment Manufacturer's "3 Horizons of Digital Transformation" journey might look like:

- **Horizon 1** would focus on applying **descriptive** and **exploratory** analytics to the organization's existing customer, product, and operational data to understand the drivers of business performance. Horizon 1 would integrate the resulting customer, product, and operational insights (propensities) with an operational framework (like Six Sigma given this is a manufacturer) to optimize operational use cases such as zero unplanned operational downtime, predictive maintenance, resource scheduling, asset utilization, "first-time fix" management, demand forecasting, energy optimization, waste minimization, fraud/theft reduction, and inventory optimization. However, with the changing market dynamics and the creation of new business models from start-ups, being the most efficient Horizon 1 manufacturer is no longer sufficient. Focusing on "paving the cow path" with **Descriptive** and **Exploratory** analytics is a great way to ensure irrelevance in Horizon 2.

- **Horizon 2** would be about architecting and delivering on the promise of "**Digital Farms**". Horizon 2 would couple Design Thinking (to understand the customers'—and potentially customers' customers'—sources of value creation) with data science (to codify the customer, product, and operational insights (propensities)) to create a "Digital Farming" business model that monetizes equipment, worker, soil, crop, weather, commodities pricing, and economic and operational insights. Horizon 2 would focus on "**digitalizing**" the farm; integrating customer, product, and operational insights (propensities) with new digital technologies such as IoT, robotic process automation, 5G, augmented reality, virtual reality, 3D printing, and blockchain to replace or augment human-intensive tasks. These new digital technologies unleash high volumes of new customer, product, and operational data that could be mined with AI, ML, and DL to uncover new customer, product, and operational insights (propensities) that can be further monetized. The Agricultural Equipment Manufacturer at Horizon 2 would create Analytic Profiles or Digital Twins of key operational entities such as tractors, farming equipment, compressors, livestock, workers, and technicians to dramatically improve, accelerate, and augment operational decision making with fine-grained, hyper-individualized **predictive** and **prescriptive** analytics.

- **Horizon 3** would be about the creation of a continuously learning and adapting "**Autonomous Farming**" business model. In Horizon 3, our Agricultural Equipment Manufacturer would master **automation** and **autonomous** analytics to create continuously learning and adapting (autonomous) products, services, and policies that adapt and evolve with minimal human intervention, to exploit superior customer, supplier, equipment, worker, soil, crop, weather, commodities, economic, and operational insights (propensities) to disrupt competitors' business models, re-engineer industry value chains, and disintermediate competitors' customer relationships.

Horizon 3, and ultimately Digital Transformation, is about reinventing and re-innovating your business model, not just simply "paving the cow path" by re-engineering your existing business processes. Sorry, but that's just shuffling the chairs on the Titanic.

Summary

Evolutions are nice and safe (unless you are the dodo bird). Revolutions, on the other hand, totally disrupt business models while seeking to disintermediate competitors' customer relationships and reinvent industry value chains. To survive the revolution, organizations must seek to reinvent how they create new sources of customer, product, and operational value. If you want to exploit the "8 Laws of Digital Transformation," organizationally, that means:

- Transitioning from siloed business functions to interdisciplinary collaboration.

- Moving from seniority-based, leader-driven decision making to data and analytics-driven decision-making at the front lines of customer engagement and operational execution.

- Transforming from a rigid and risk-averse culture, to an agile, experimental, learning, and adaptable culture.

- Becoming value-driven within the frame of customer journey centricity.

Now we are ready to move to the final chapter, which covers the single most important determinant of your organization's digital transformation success...your organizational culture and team empowerment. While it's been famously said that "software is eating the world," in the end, culture eats everything. But first, some more homework.

Further Reading

1. *Evan Tarver, What Are the Primary Activities of Michael Porter's Value Chain?, Investopedia*, May 26, 2019: `https://www.investopedia.com/ask/answers/050115/what-are-primary-activities-michael-porters-value-chain.asp`

2. *McKinsey & Company, Enduring Ideas: The three horizons of growth*, December 1, 2009: `https://www.mckinsey.com/business-functions/strategy-and-corporate-finance/our-insights/enduring-ideas-the-three-horizons-of-growth`

3. *Geoffrey Moore, "Zone to Win: Organizing to Compete in an Age of Disruption,"* 2015

Homework

1. Does your organization differentiate between Digitalization and Digital Transformation?

Some progress with Digitalization	Harvest Digitalization data & insights	Digitalization path to Digital Transformation	Embed Digitalization insights in DX journey

1	2	3	4	5	6	7	8	9	10

Score:_____ Assessment: _____

_____

_____

_____

2. How fluent is your organization in "speaking the language of the customer?"

Execs think Design Thinking is a fad	Design Thinking experiments are happening	Design Thinking CXO Sponsor	Organizational standardized on Design Thinking

1	2	3	4	5	6	7	8	9	10

Score:_____ Assessment: _____

_____
_____
_____

3. Where does your organization sit on the Analytics Maturity Curve?

Some Predictive analytics	Integrating Predictive & Prescriptive	Exploring Autonomous Pilots	Autonomous Assets are part of the strategic initiative

1	2	3	4	5	6	7	8	9	10

Score:_____ Assessment: _____

_____
_____
_____

4. What is the status of your "3 Horizons of Digital Transformation" journey?

Make Horizon 1 investments to benefit Horizon 2	Make Horizon 2 investments to benefit Horizon 1	Make Horizon 3 investments to benefit 1 & 2	Thrive in Horizon 3. What's Horizon 1?

1	2	3	4	5	6	7	8	9	10

Score:_____ Assessment: _____

_____

_____

_____

BILL SCHMARZO
Dean of Big Data

9

CREATING A CULTURE OF INNOVATION THROUGH EMPOWERMENT

Digital Transformation is the creation of a continuously learning and adapting business model (AI-driven and human-empowered) that seeks to identify, codify, and operationalize actionable customer, product, and operational insights (propensities) in order to optimize (reinvent) operational efficiency, enhance customer value creation, mitigate operational and compliance risk, and create new revenue opportunities.

Okay, now that we've covered all the economics, data, and analytics mumble jumble, let's focus on the real secret sauce to any digital transformation journey—empowering your people.

This will be the most difficult chapter in the book because it forces the reader to embrace a very uncomfortable and even troubling concept—ambiguity. Ambiguity—the quality of being open to more than one interpretation—is the key to human, societal, and organizational evolution. If everyone has the same perspectives and same opinions—if our thinking is just a clone of everyone else's thinking—then evolution is over, and humankind and society are doomed.

This chapter will be uncomfortable because everyone desires to work with people just like themselves. It's easier and more comfortable when everyone you work with has the same perspectives. But that's a formula for stagnation and at worst, groupthink.

So, this chapter, first and foremost, is about creating a culture that encourages diversity of perspectives but also seeks to empower teams to embrace and exploit this diversity of perspectives to drive the innovation necessary to achieve digital transformation.

But first, a history lesson.

Team Empowerment History Lesson

In the 1805 Battle of Trafalgar, British Admiral Lord Nelson faced the superior forces of the combined French and Spanish naval Armada. The French and Spanish naval Armada was determined to clear a path for Napoleon to invade England, and only Lord Nelson stood in their way. Lord Nelson was badly outnumbered and outgunned, so he needed to *reframe* his battle strategy to overcome these debilitating disadvantages.

In 1805, the standard method of naval warfare involved ships lining up parallel to each other to maximize the effectiveness of their cannons. Naval battle in the "Age of Sail" was a simple game of math—firing cannonballs more quickly than your opponent was the best way to ensure victory. Yes, the **Key Performance Indicator** (**KPI**) for naval battle success could have been "shots per minute" based on the number of cannons and the crew's ability for rapid reloading.

Given his predicament, Lord Nelson decided on a different naval engagement strategy. Instead of the traditional parallel arrangement, he arranged his ships perpendicularly into two columns and drove them directly into the opponent's line. This approach, captured in *Figure 9.1*, would minimize the enemy's firepower advantage (less exposed surface area for Lord Nelson's fleet in which to endure more cannon damage) while driving a wedge between the enemy's command line. Once the enemy's line was broken, Lord Nelson's ships could fire point blank into the Armada, causing absolute chaos in the process.

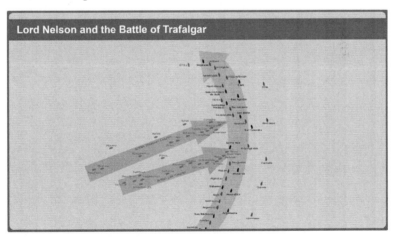

Figure 9.1: Lord Nelson and the Battle of Trafalgar Battle Strategy

While much credit for Lord Nelson's overwhelming success in the naval battle was given to his innovative battle strategy, an important key to his success was how he empowered each of his ship captains to operate independently and "think on their own during the heat of battle," turning them into "entrepreneurs of battle."

On the opposite side of the battle, the French and Spanish Armada were commanded by Vice Admiral Pierre-Charles de Villeneuve and Admiral Don Federico Gravina. They used the traditional, centralized command-and-control structure to send battle instructions (using flags) to the Armada ship captains with instructions on how to proceed during the battle.

Lord Nelson exploited his decentralized, empowered team approach to pierce the Armada's line of attack, thereby defeating the centralized command-and-control structure of the French and Spanish Armada. In fact, Lord Nelson's captains were successful in winning the battle even though he was killed during the battle.

So, what can your organization learn from Lord Nelson and the Battle of Trafalgar?

If you want to win the Digital Transformation game, spend the time and management effort to empower your teams so that your organization can defeat entrenched competitors and lead your organization's digital transformation charge (and hopefully your CEO doesn't get killed during the battle).

Empowering your teams at the front lines of customer engagement and operational execution will likely have more impact on the organization's digital transformation success than the strategizing and pontificating of senior management. So, here are some tips on how to empower those teams.

Empowerment #1: Internalize the Organization's Mission

Gaining buy-in to the organization's Mission Statement requires that everyone be able to internalize what that mission statement means to them, their jobs, and their personal principles.

Make sure that everyone in the organization—and I mean E-V-E-R-Y-O-N-E—understands the organization's **Mission Statement** (and it will help to have a simple-to-understand one). A **Mission Statement** should not be long (it should pass the 30-second elevator test) and not contain non-descript, non-committal weasel words. A Mission Statement should clearly articulate why an organization exists.

Here are some of my favorites:

- **TED**: Spread ideas.
- **JetBlue**: To inspire humanity—both in the air and on the ground.
- **American Heart Association**: To be a relentless force for a world of longer, healthier lives.
- **Patagonia**: Build the best product, cause no unnecessary harm, use business to inspire and implement solutions to the environmental crisis.
- **Nordstrom**: To give customers the most compelling shopping experience possible.
- **LinkedIn**: Create economic opportunity for every member of the global workforce.
- **Starbucks**: To inspire and nurture the human spirit—one person, one cup and one neighborhood at a time.

I suspect Lord Nelson's mission statement was probably simple and to the point: "Don't let those suckers break through the line otherwise we're going to be eating baguettes instead of fish and chips." Okay, a bit long but I bet it was something like that.

Everybody in the organization should not only be able to articulate the organization's mission statement but be able to express how the mission statement impacts their day-to-day jobs, as well as what that mission statement means to them personally.

Empowerment #2: Speak the Language of the Customer

Speaking the Language of the Customer ensures that everyone not only has the same customer-centricity focus but speak the same language that the customer uses (that is, avoids internal acronyms and buzzwords).

Establish a common language so that everyone uses the same words to describe the same goals, assets, and actions. To institutionalize the *"language of the customer"* in your organization, I recommend embracing the empowering and innovative discipline of **Design Thinking**.

Design Thinking is a customer-centric discipline that necessitates an open and collaborative mindset that leverages facilitated ideation techniques and tools to discover and validate unmet customer needs within the context and constraints of a specific customer problem or opportunity.

Design Thinking is a highly iterative yet scalable process that starts by:

- **Empathizing** with the targeted customer's challenge.

- **Defining** or framing the customer's challenge.

- **Ideating** potential solutions (where all ideas are worthy of consideration).

- **Prototyping** different solution options (to validate *with* the customers in order to learn *from* the customers).

- **Testing**, **learning**, and **refining** until you find a workable solution (see *Figure 9.2*).

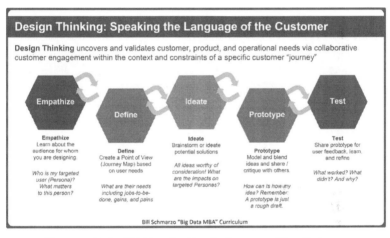

Figure 9.2: Design Thinking: Speaking the Language of Your Customers

Persona profiles (to personalize the customer's challenge), customer journey maps (to understand the customer's journey towards a solution), and stakeholder maps (with personal win conditions for each stakeholder) are just a few the Design Thinking tools and techniques that you can use to understand your customers, their jobs, the value propositions, and their associated gains (benefits) and pains (impediments).

Empowerment #3: Empowering Teams Through Organizational Improvisation

Organizational Improvisation yields flexible and malleable teams that can maintain operational integrity while morphing the team's structure and execution in response to the changing needs of the situation.

Like a great soccer team (think of the United States Women's World Cup championship soccer team...like watching ballet on the soccer field) or an enthralling jazz ensemble (like Miles Davis or Freddie Hubbard...since I did play jazz trumpet in college), successful organizations embrace **Organizational Improvisation** or improv. They exhibit the ability to morph the team's structure and operating plans in real-time in response to changing customer and/ or operational conditions while maintaining operational integrity.

Teams win games and change the world, not individuals. Yes, there are individuals (Thomas Edison, Alexander Graham Bell, Steve Jobs, Bill Gates, Elon Musk) who can evangelize an aspirational vision, but in the end, **Empowered Teams** win the game. To master empowering teams, we must empower organizational improv.

So how do we cultivate empowered teams that can morph in the heat of battle while driving the organization's digital transformation forward within a constantly changing environment? Learn to play video games!

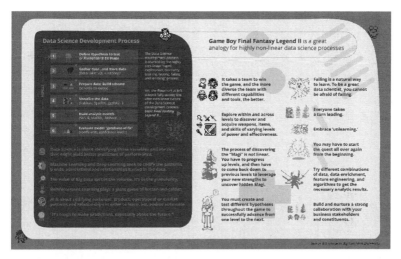

Figure 9.3: Why Data Science Team Development is like playing Final Fantasy Legend II!

The Game Boy© Final Fantasy Legend II™ game (which I have defeated several times) is a surprisingly fabulous management tool that yields several valuable lessons in creating empowered teams, including:

- **It takes a team to win the game**. The more diverse the team, with different perspectives, capabilities, and tools, the better. Build your team based upon potential capabilities rather than on current capabilities. Invest in the future. For example, while the robot is powerful in the earlier levels of the game and will single-handedly win lots of early battles, it eventually tops out and becomes ineffective at the later, more challenging levels.

- **Discovery is a highly non-linear process**. The path to discovery is not a straight line. There will be times where you will need to double back to previous levels to gather important items (and insights) that you were not capable of gathering or learning before.

- **You must test different hypotheses throughout the game to find the ones that win**. You can't measure success by the number of hours played. Just playing the game more doesn't help you win the game. Progress and success are achieved by successfully defining, testing, proving, and advancing hypothesis by hypothesis, where the learnings from the successful completion of one hypothesis guides the development of the next hypothesis.

- **Failing is a natural way to learn**. You will learn and get stronger with each interaction, but you will also fail at times along your journey. But failures provide a learning opportunity to better understand the deficiencies that you and your team need to address. *If you aren't failing enough, then you're not learning enough.*

- **Everyone takes a turn leading**. There are certain situations where the wizard must lead, and other situations where an imp might have to lead, and others where the human must lead. Everyone on the team must be prepared to lead depending on the situation. Be sure that everyone on your team has been trained and coached so that they are prepared to lead successfully when their time comes.

- **Embrace "unlearning."** Just when you think you have developed the necessary skills and capabilities, then you battle a boss monster and realize that all your planning to win that battle was inadequate (as Mike Tyson once said "everyone has a plan until they get punched in the face"). The capabilities that help to overcome one obstacle may be totally irrelevant to the next obstacle. Be prepared to let go of outdated approaches to learn new ones.

- **Be prepared to start all over**. You may find in the later levels of your journey that the team you have assembled and the capabilities that you have gained are insufficient for winning the final level. Sometimes your current strategy just tops out, and you need to morph the team to include different perspectives, capabilities, and experiences. *Hint: that's the importance and power of nurturing organizational improvisation.*

- **Embrace diversity of perspectives**. Be prepared to blend, bend, and break apart different perspectives to overcome certain challenges. And surprise, sometimes it's the combinations that you least expected that yield the most valuable and actionable insights.

- **Nurture strong collaboration across the ecosystem**. Finally, there will be many annoying and some very evil creatures along that path who are trying to hinder, slow down, or kill your journey (just normal life in the corporate world). Build and nurture a strong collaboration across all of your constituents who can guide you and can even help you to win battles at critical points on the journey.

So, dust off that old Game Boy and learn how to empower your teams!

 DEAN OF BIG DATA TIP:

There is a big difference between **Opinions** and **Perspectives**. Opinions are statements about something, but not necessarily based on fact or knowledge. Asking for one's **Opinion** on a topic is unproductive.

However, asking for one's **Perspective** on a topic can yield the rationale behind one's opinion, and in that rationale, you might find some nuggets around which to collaborate.

Empowerment #4: Embrace an "AND" Mentality

"AND" Mentality embraces differing perspectives to blend, bend, and break apart the different ideas to create something more powerful and more empowering than what was there before.

Another history lesson (I always loved history in middle school): If you had challenged car manufacturers in 1979 to increase horsepower while also improving mileage per car, the automobile executives would have looked at you like you had lobsters crawling out of your ears. However, that is exactly what happened.

The car manufacturers in the 1970s operated with an "OR" mentality—customers could have cars with good "fuel mileage OR horsepower" but not both. However, the automobile industry was forced to reframe this mindset when the U.S. government mandated higher vehicle fuel mileage in 1975 and then again in 2007. And instead of going out of business, car manufacturers (or at least some of them—I'm looking at you, Hummer) embraced the dilemma and ended up both improving fuel mileage AND increasing horsepower through a number of product design, development, and manufacturing innovations (see *Figure 9.4*).

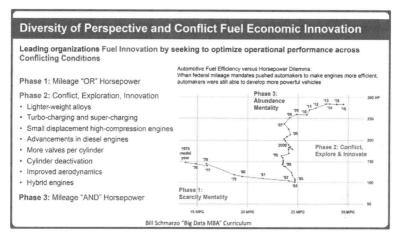

Figure 9.4: Economic Transformation of the Automobile Industry

As we discussed in *Chapter 3, A Review of Basic Economic Concepts*, when we talked about transforming the organization's **Economic Value Curve**, sometimes a crisis can create the necessary impetus for organizations to move beyond an "OR" mentality and embrace an "AND" mentality to survive.

Organizations that are seeking to drive their digital transformation must replace their "OR" mentality with an "AND" mentality. This is difficult but necessary because getting organizational alignment on the best path forward on critical product, market, or organizational decisions is overly challenging. Typically, product-centric organizations engage in "wear them down" decision-making techniques that end up defaulting to the Least "Worst Option" that offends the fewest stakeholders. Stakeholders just get worn out by the continuous debate and finally folks just start giving in to the endless debate ("Nobody is right when everyone is wrong"). This "lowest common denominator" approach leads to sub-optimal decisions from the perspective of both the organization as well as the customers.

To overcome this dilemma, organizations must embrace an "AND" mentality that merges the product-centric AND the customer-centric perspectives to synergize a better solution. Be prepared to blend, bend, and break apart the different perspectives to discover the essence of each perspective: **blend** two or more loosely coupled perspectives into a new perspective, **bend** an original perspective from a multitude of different dimensions to see what new perspectives it yields, and finally **break apart** a perspective into its subcomponents to rearrange, eliminate, or re-engineer the perspective subcomponents into something greater than before.

When internal stakeholders with diverse perspectives can identify, understand, and empathize with their customers while at the same time frame those customer needs from the perspective of products, organizations can transform their operational decision making from the **Least "Worst Option"** to the **Best "Best Option"** (see *Figure 9.5*).

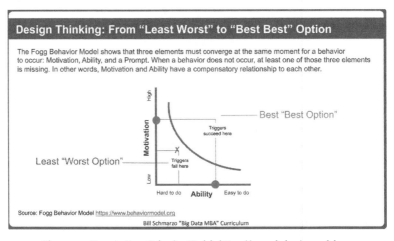

Figure 9.5: Source: Fogg Behavior Model: https://www.behaviormodel.org

Organizations can transition from **Least "Worst Options"** towards **Best "Best Options"** by decomposing everyone's perspectives into the **assets** that make up those perspectives. These assets may include product capabilities, market insights, customer relationships, or personal skills. After you have decomposed everyone's perspectives into these assets, then blend and bend different combinations of assets to create the **Best "Best Option"** to which everyone can contribute and support.

You'll be surprised how enlightening and fun this process can be when you empower teams to transform everyone's different perspectives into the assets that can be combined in new, more innovative solutions.

Empowerment #5: Embrace Critical Thinking

Critical Thinking is the judicious and objective analysis, exploration, and evaluation of an issue or a subject to form a viable and justifiable judgment.

Teaching my university students to embrace critical thinking is crucial for creating our future business and civic leaders. Likewise, it is also crucial for achieving digital transformation. Here is what I expect of my students with respect to mastering critical thinking:

1. **Never accept the initial answer as the right answer**. It's too easy to take the initial result and think that it's good enough. But good enough is usually *not good enough,* and one needs to invest the time and effort to explore if there is a better "good enough" answer.

2. **Be skeptical**. Never accept someone's "statement of opinion" as "fact." Learn to question what you read or hear. It's very easy to accept at face value whatever someone tells you, but that's a sign of a lazy mind. And learn to discern facts from opinions. You know what they say about opinions...

3. **Consider the source**. When you are gathering requirements, consider the credibility, experience, and maybe most importantly, the agenda of the source. Not all sources are of equal value, and the credibility of the source is highly dependent upon the context of the situation.

4. **Don't get happy ears**. Don't listen for the answer that you want to hear. Instead, listen with the intent to learn. *Tomorrow's leaders won't seek out information to confirm; they'll seek out information to learn.*

5. **Embrace struggling**. The easy answer isn't always the right answer. In fact, the easy answer is seldom the right answer, especially when it comes to complex situations that we face in society and the business world.

6. **Stay curious; have an insatiable appetite to learn**. This is especially true in a world where technologies are changing so rapidly. Curiosity may have killed the cat, but I wouldn't want a cat making decisions for me anyway (otherwise we'd have a steady diet of dead mice).

7. **Apply the reasonableness test**. Is what you are reading making sense from what you have seen or read elsewhere (sorry, the Pope didn't vote in the US election)? While technologies are changing so rapidly, societal norms and ethics aren't. Do you understand the difference between "Do no harm" versus "Do good"? If not, then reread the Parable of the Good Samaritan.

8. **Pause to think**. Find a quiet place where you can sequester yourself to really think about everything that you've pulled together. Take a deep breath and the time to contemplate before rushing to the answer.

9. **Conflict is good...and necessary**. Life is full of tradeoffs that requires striking a delicate balance between numerous competing factors (increase one factor while reducing another). As we discussed earlier, these types of conflicts are the fuel for innovation.

Critical thinking...geez, wish more people were practicing that art.

Summary

Lord Nelson empowered ship captains who were "entrepreneurs of battle" by creating agile, malleable teams that could collaborate, share, and learn, based upon a common mission, shared language, and a culture of trust, openness, and fearlessness. Organizations that are seeking to achieve their digital transformation must also empower "entrepreneurs of innovation" by creating agile, malleable teams that can collaborate, share, and learn, based upon a common mission, a shared language of the customer, and a culture of team empowerment.

My final point in the book is this: You have all the tools and skills necessary to be successful, but ultimately your success is on you. The minute you start to blame others for your problems, you abdicate control of your life. Don't do it. Own your mistakes, and you will own your future.

I have failed several times in my life, and each failure has not only tested my faith and resolve but has provided valuable lessons that I could carry forward to the next chapter of my life. I hope your failures can also fuel your future successes (see *Figure 9.6*).

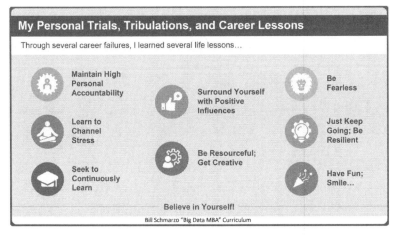

Figure 9.6: My Personal Trials and Tribulations

Again, own your mistakes, and you will own your future. That's the key to anyone's empowered, innovative, and transformational journey.

Further Reading

1. *GroupThink*: https://en.wikipedia.org/wiki/Groupthink

2. *Age of Sail*: https://en.wikipedia.org/wiki/Age_of_Sail

3. *Battle of Trafalgar*: https://en.wikipedia.org/wiki/Order_of_battle_at_the_Battle_of_Trafalgar

4. *Kyle Stock* and *David Ingold, America's Cars Are Suddenly Getting Faster and More Efficient,* 17 May 2017: https://www.bloomberg.com/news/features/2017-05-17/america-s-cars-are-all-fast-and-furious-these-days

Homework

1. How well do you understand and speak the language of your customers?

Not clear who our "Customer" is	Created Personas and Customer Journey Maps	Have prototyped solutions with Customers	Co-created and deployed solutions with Customers

1	2	3	4	5	6	7	8	9	10

Score:_____ Assessment: _____

_____

_____

2. How are you removing impediments and empowering organizational improvements?

Rigid command and control structure	Cross-functional teams for special projects only	Collaborative culture within functional cost centers	Teams empowered to morph as needed

1	2	3	4	5	6	7	8	9	10

Score:_____ Assessment: _____

_____

_____

3. How are you building an "AND" culture around personal accountability?

Senior Execs makes all the decisions	Settle for Least "Worst Options"	Selective team empowerment	Empowered to drive towards Best "Best Option"

1	2	3	4	5	6	7	8	9	10

Score:_____ Assessment: _____

_____

_____

_____

BILL SCHMARZO
Dean of Big Data

Appendix A

My Most Popular Economics of Data, Analytics, and Digital Transformation Infographics

The world is constantly evolving. Technology continues to change how we think, communicate, learn, and adapt. Our culture is hungry for knowledge, efficiencies, breakthroughs, and the sharing of such, which is largely consumed by the ever-proliferating platforms of social media. **Infographics**, visualizations of concepts, are enabling individuals to quickly gain insights and make practical use of their meaning; a "pictorial" that's easily assimilated as we navigate through today's endless sea of data.

In the last year, I have relied heavily on the use of infographics to complement my keynotes, customer discussions, classroom lectures, and blogs—pertaining to the economics of data, analytics, AI, design thinking, and digital transformation—due to the tool's succinct way of summarizing and conveying a particular concept. In fact, my infographics have been so well-received at translating my thoughts and ideas into easily assimilated morsels that I now consider myself an infographic-making junky!

I've learned that a *good* infographic provides an interesting visual. However, a *great* infographic tells a story, orchestrated in such a way as to convey a deep and sometimes complicated message in an entertaining and engaging manner. There are lots of details in the infographics that I'm featuring in this appendix, but to leave out these details would greatly shortchange that story you are about to experience.

So, consume the power of these infographics, and I'd love to hear from you as my most important critic and colleague!

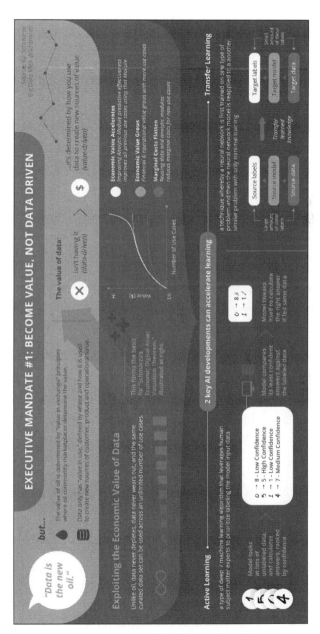

Figure 10.1: Become Value Driven infographic

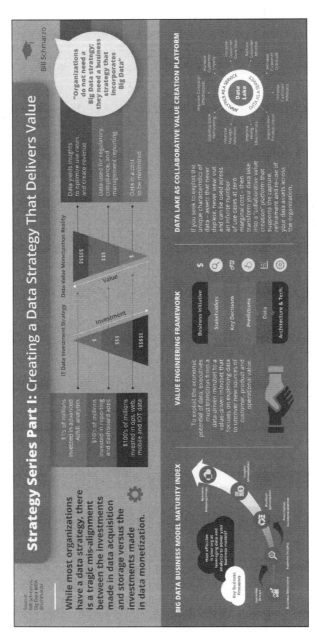

Figure 10.2: Creating a Data Strategy that Delivers Value infographic

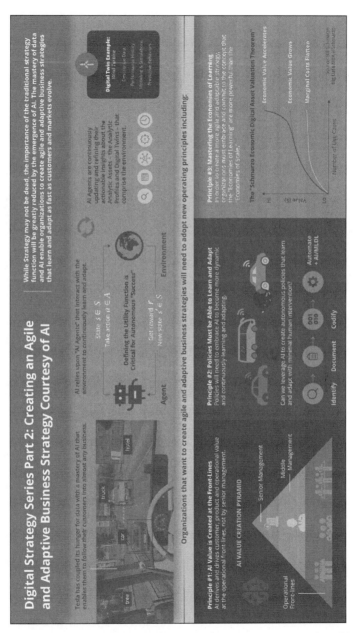

Figure 10.3: Creating an Agile and Adaptive Business Strategy Using AI infographic

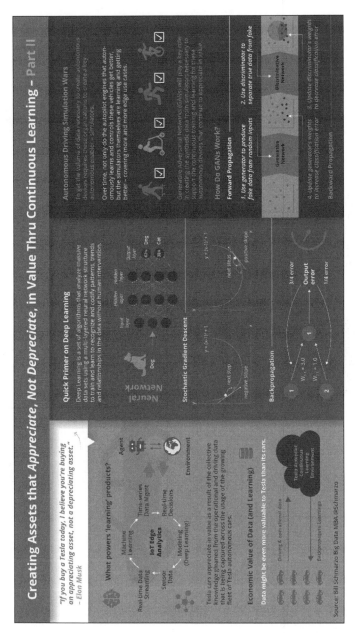

Figure 10.4: Creating Assets that Appreciate in Value infographic

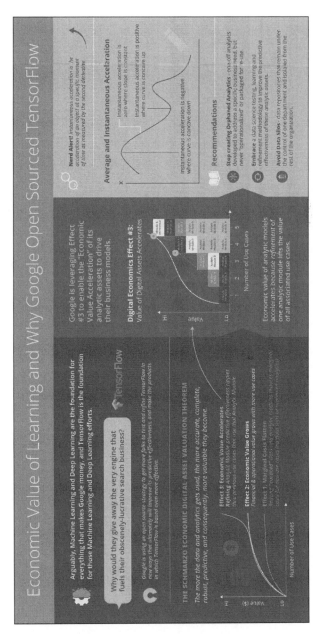

Figure 10.5: Economic Value infographic

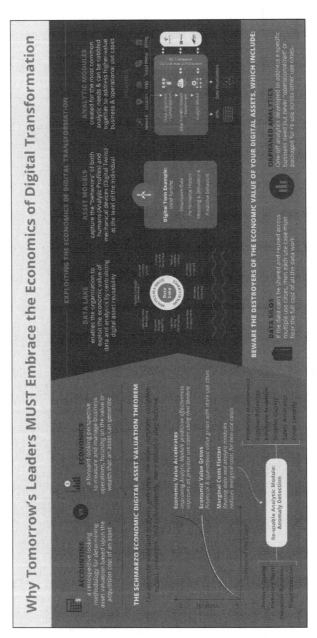

Figure 10.6: Embrace the Economics of Data Transformation infographic

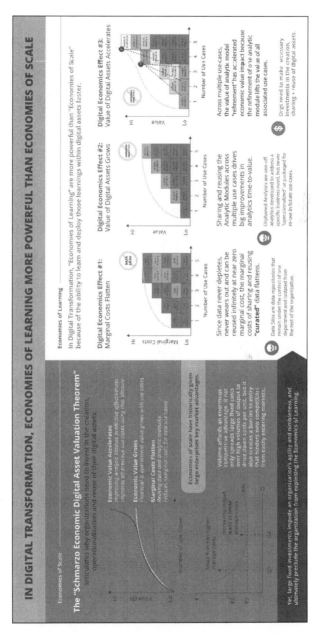

Figure 10.7: Economies of Learning are More Powerful Than Economies of Scale infographic

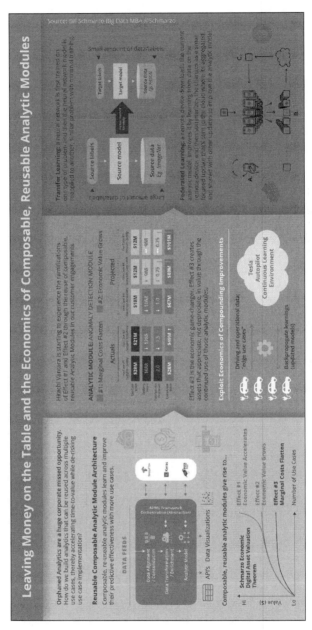

Figure 10.8: Leaving Money on the Table and Reusable Analytics infographic

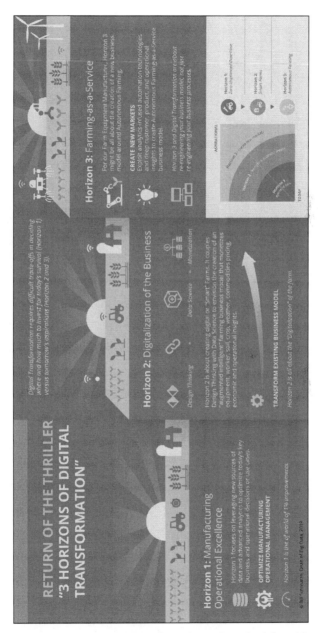

Figure 10.9: The Three Horizons of Digital Transformation infographic

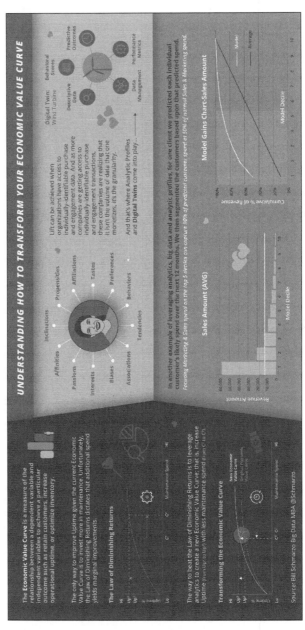

Figure 10.10: Understanding How to Transform Your Economic Value Curve infographic

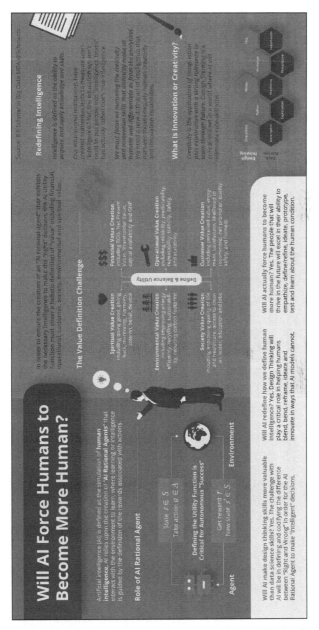

Figure 10.11: Will AI Force Humans to Become More Human? infographic

Appendix B

The Economics of Data, Analytics, and Digital Transformation Cheat Sheet

I am offering this cheat sheet as a quick way to summarize the key takeaways from each chapter of the book. While these brief points won't replace the need to read the book, they might help in providing a quick reference and pointer to where the takeaways were covered in the book. Enjoy!

Chapter 1: The CEO Mandate: Become Value-driven, Not Data-driven

- "Data is the new oil" in that the way that oil fueled the economic growth of the 20th century, data will be the catalyst for the economic growth in the 21st century.

- If "data is the new oil," then how effective is your organization at leveraging data and analytics to power your business model?

- Data may be the new oil, but it is the customer, product, and operational analytic insights buried in the data that will determine the winners and losers in the 21st century.

- Crossing the "Analytics Chasm" requires organizations to leverage the economics of data and analytics on a use case-by-use case basis.

- Data science is about identifying variables and metrics that might be better predictors of performance.

Chapter 2: Value Engineering: The Secret Sauce for Data Science Success

- Value Engineering starts with what's important ($$) to the organization.

- While the decisions have not changed over the years, what has changed—courtesy of advanced analytics—are the answers.

- Organizations don't fail due to a lack of use cases; they fail because they have too many.

- Most Digital Transformation journeys don't fail because of technology issues; they get thwarted by passive-aggressive behaviors.

- A diverse set of stakeholders is critical because they provide different perspectives on variables and metrics against which data science progress and success will be measured.

- The heart of the Data Science Value Engineering Framework is the collaboration with the different stakeholders to identify, validate, value, and prioritize the key decisions (use cases).

Chapter 3: A Review of Basic Economic Concepts

- **Economics** is a branch of knowledge concerned with the production, consumption, and transfer of wealth; economics is about the creation of value.

- The **Economic Value Curve** is a measure of the relationship between a dependent variable and independent variables to achieve a particular business or operational outcome.

- **Analytic Modules** are composable, reusable, continuously learning analytic assets that deliver predefined business or operational outcomes.

- The **Law of Diminishing Returns** is a measure of the decrease in the marginal output of production as the amount of a single factor of production (input) is incrementally increased.

- The **Economic Multiplier Effect** refers to the increase in final income arising from any new injection of spending.

- **Marginal Propensity to Consume** (**MPC**) measures the impact of a change in output (production) as a ratio to the change in input (investment).

- **Utility** refers to the perceived value received from the consumption or use of a good or service.

- **Scarcity** refers to limitations—insufficient resources, goods, or abilities—to achieve the desired end. Optimizing decisions about how to make the best use of scarce resources is a fundamental economics challenge.

- **Postponement Theory** is a decision to postpone a decision. Postponement occurs when one party seeks to either gain additional information and/or to delay the decision in search of better terms.

- **Efficiency** is a relationship between ends and means. When we call a situation inefficient, we are claiming that we could achieve the desired ends with fewer means, or that the means employed could produce more of the desired ends.

- **Price Elasticity** of demand is the quantitative measure of consumer behavior that indicates the quantity of demand for a product or service depending on its increase or decrease in price.

Chapter 4: University of San Francisco Economic Value of Data Research Paper

- Accounting is a "Value in Exchange" asset valuation methodology; that is, the value of an asset is determined by what someone is willing to pay for that asset.

- Economics is a "Value in Use" asset valuation methodology; that is, the value of an asset is determined by the value generated using that asset.

- A data lake can be transformed into a "collaborative value creation" platform by facilitating the capture, refinement, and reuse of the organization's data and analytic assets across multiple use cases.

Chapter 5: The Economic Value of Data Theorems

- **The Data Economic Multiplier Effect**: Data never wears out, never depletes, and can be used across an unlimited number of use cases at near-zero marginal cost.

- **Theorem #1**: It isn't the data itself that's valuable; it's the trends, patterns, and relationships gleaned from the data about your customers, products, and operations that are valuable.

- **Theorem #2**: It is from the quantification of the trends, patterns, and relationships that drive predictions about what is likely to happen.

- **Theorem #3**: Predictions drive monetization opportunities through improved business and operational use cases.

- **Theorem #4**: The ability to reuse the same datasets across multiple use cases is the real economic game-changer.

- **Theorem #5**: Trying to optimize across a diverse set of objectives can yield more granular, higher fidelity outcomes that enable "doing more with less".

Chapter 6: The Economics of Artificial Intelligence

- Using Artificial Intelligence, you can create assets that appreciate in value, not depreciate, the more that these assets are used.

- "Orphaned Analytics" are one-off analytics developed to address a specific business need but are never "operationalized" or packaged for reuse across the organization.

- **Deep Learning** is a set of algorithms that analyze massive datasets using a multi-layered neural network structure, where each layer comprises numerous nodes, to train and learn to recognize and codify patterns, trends, and relationships buried in the data...without human intervention.

- **Reinforcement Learning** is a class of machine learning algorithm that seeks to "learn" by taking actions within a controlled environment with the goal to maximize rewards while minimizing costs.

- **Transfer Learning** is a technique whereby one neural network is first trained on one type of problem and then reapplied to another similar problem with minimal training.

- **Artificial Intelligence** (**AI**) relies upon "AI Agents" that interact with the environment to learn and adapt, where learning is guided by the definition of the rewards and penalties associated with each action.

- **An AI Utility Function** provides the objective criterion that measures the progress and success of an AI rational agent's actions.

- The Power of Compounding a 1% improvement compounded 365 times equals a 37.8x overall improvement ($1.01 \wedge 365 = 37.78$).

- **Autonomous Law #1**: Autonomous entities need lots of real-time, granular data from a robust and diverse set of use cases against which to learn using AI and Deep Reinforcement Learning techniques.

- **Autonomous Law #2**: Autonomous entities leverage fail-safe environments (simulators) to train the AI Agents to operate, learn, and adapt across a wide variety of use cases.

- **Autonomous Law #3**: Autonomous entities are complex systems comprising sometimes conflicting subsystems that are seeking to optimize their own performance.

- **Autonomous Law #4**: For an entity to be autonomous, that entity must integrate, interoperate, and optimize across all of these subsystems to achieve its AI Utility Function with minimal human intervention.

- **Autonomous Law #5**: Autonomous projects won't fail because of the AI technologies, they'll fail because of a poorly constructed AI Utility Function.

- If you want to change the game, you need to change your frame.

Chapter 7: The Schmarzo Economic Digital Asset Valuation Theorem

- "Economies of Learning" are more powerful than "Economies of Scale".

- A use case-by-use case deployment approach exploits the "Economies of Learning" through the rapid learning and reapplication of those learnings to future use cases.

- **The Schmarzo Economic Digital Asset Valuation Theorem** leverages the unique economic characteristics of data and analytics to increase organizational value via three "effects".

- **Digital Economics Effect #1**: Since data never depletes, never wears out, and can be reused against an unlimited number of use cases at near-zero marginal cost, reusing "curated" data and analytic modules reduce the marginal costs of new use cases.

- Data silos are the killers of the economic value of data.

- **Digital Economics Effect #2**: Sharing and reusing the data and analytic modules accelerate use case time-to-value and de-risks use case implementation.

- **Digital Economics Effect #3**: Analytic module "refinement" accelerates economic value because the continuous improvements of a specific analytic module lift the value of all use cases that used that same analytic module.

Chapter 8: The 8 Laws of Digital Transformation

- Digital Transformation Laws are statements based on repeated observations that describe or predict a range of natural phenomena.
- **Digital Transformation Law #1**: Digital Transformation is about reinventing and innovating business models, not just optimizing existing business processes.
- **Digital Transformation Law #2**: Digital Transformation is about reinventing your customer engagements and business operations with continuously learning AI capabilities to derive and drive new sources of customer, product, service, and operational value.
- **Digital Transformation Law #3**: Digital Transformation is about reinventing your business model to expand upon, exploit, and monetize those sources of customer value creation while eliminating the inhibitors of value creation.
- **Digital Transformation Law #4**: Digital Transformation is about creating new digital assets that leverage customer, product, and operational insights to drive granular decisions and hyper-individualized prescriptive recommendations
- **Digital Transformation Law #5**: Digital Transformation is about predicting what's likely to happen, prescribing recommended actions, and continuously learning and adapting faster than your competition.

- **Digital Transformation Law #6**: AI can enable more relevant operational and policy decisions by continuously learning and adapting based upon most current environment situations... with minimal human intervention.

- **Digital Transformation Law #7**: The heart of Digital Transformation is the ability to identify, codify, and operationalize the sources of customer, product, and operational value within an environment that is continuously learning and adapting to ever-changing customer and market needs.

- **Digital Transformation Law #8**: Create an Aspirational Vision to focus and prioritize the organization's immediate and long-term investments in customer, product, and operational value creation.

Chapter 9: Creating a Culture of Innovation Through Empowerment

- Ambiguity—the quality of being open to more than one interpretation—is the key to human, society and organizational evolution.

- Empowering your teams at the front line of customer engagement and operational execution will have more impact on the organization's digital transformation success than the strategizing and pontificating of senior management.

- **Empowerment #1:** Gaining buy-in to the organization's Mission Statement requires everyone to internalize what that mission statement means to them, their jobs, and their personal principles.

- **Empowerment #2:** Speaking the Language of the Customer ensures that everyone not only has the same customer-centricity focus but is speaking the same language that the customer uses.

- **Empowerment #3**: Organizational Improvisation yields flexible and malleable teams that can maintain operational integrity while morphing the team's structure and execution in response to the changing needs of the situation.

- **Empowerment #4**: "AND" Mentality embraces differing perspectives to blend, bend, and break apart different ideas to synergize something more powerful and more empowering than what was there before.

- **Empowerment #5**: Critical Thinking is the judicious and objective analysis, exploration, and evaluation of an issue or a subject to form a viable and justifiable judgment.

- Own your mistakes, and you will own your future.

OTHER BOOKS YOU MAY ENJOY

If you enjoyed this book, you may be interested in this book by Packt:

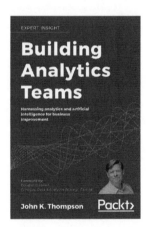

Building Analytics Team
John K. Thompson
ISBN: 978-1-80020-316-7

- Avoid organizational and technological pitfalls of moving from a defined project to a production environment

- Enable team members to focus on higher-value work and tasks

- Build Advanced Analytics and Artificial Intelligence (AA&AI) functions in an organization

- Outsource certain projects to competent and capable third parties

- Support the operational areas that intend to invest in business intelligence, descriptive statistics, and small-scale predictive analytics

- Analyze the operational area, the processes, the data, and the organizational resistance

Leave a review - let other readers know what you think

Please share your thoughts on this book with others by leaving a review on the site that you bought it from. If you purchased the book from Amazon, please leave us an honest review on this book's Amazon page. This is vital so that other potential readers can see and use your unbiased opinion to make purchasing decisions, we can understand what our customers think about our products, and our authors can see your feedback on the title that they have worked with Packt to create. It will only take a few minutes of your time, but is valuable to other potential customers, our authors, and Packt. Thank you!

Index

Persona 34
Personally Identifiable
    Information (PII) 89
Point of Sales (POS) 55
policies 162
Postponement Theory 60
Potential Data Sources
  identifying 40, 41
price elasticity 64
Principal Component Analysis
    (PCA) 95
Prioritization Matrix 37, 38
Prioritize Decisions
  uses cases 35-38
propensities 3

Q

Question 36

R

reinforcement learning 114, 115
Return on Investment
    (ROI) 15, 132

S

scarcity 58, 59
Schmarzo Economic Digital
    Asset Valuation
    Theorem 130, 162
  implementing 142
Stakeholders Personas 34
Standard Industrial
    Classification (SIC) 152
Starbucks 179

Stochastic Gradient
    Descent 113
Store Operations 79
Strategic Business Initiative
  identifying 31
  metrics, identifying 33
Sunk Costs 57
Supervised Machine
    Learning 10
Supporting Analytics
  identifying 38, 39
Supporting Architecture and
    Technologies
  identifying 41

T

team empowerment
  AND mentality 186-188
  critical thinking 189, 191
  history 176-178
  language of customer 180
  mission statement, for
    organization 179
  organizational improvisation
    182-185
TED 179
TensorFlow 118
  architecture 118
Tesla Autonomous Vehicles
    case study 120-122
Thinking Like a Data Scientist
    methodology 133
Traditional Customer
    Journey 155
transfer learning (TL) 115

U

**Unsupervised Machine
 Learning** 10
Use Case (Use_case_FV) 98
utility 65

V

value-driven mindset 2-5
Variable Costs 56